Contents

D0994192

Dedication

For D and E, from Sandi

For Holly, from Paul

Upping Sticks is also dedicated to the memory of Richard Craze, who tragically, passed away suddenly during production of this book. Rich brought fun to the otherwise dull stuff like contracts and royalties. His regular e-mail banter, humour (and chocolate) is sorely missed.

Acknowledgements

We would like to thank all the people who took the time and trouble to complete questionnaires as part of the research for this book. We would also like to thank Jeffrey Normie, of Jeffrey Normie Estate Agents (**www.jeffreynormie.co.uk**) for his input into certain sections of this book; Jeffrey has been an estate agent for over 40 years and has run his own agency for the past 26 years. He was recommended to us by a couple of his clients as a 'decent' estate agent and indeed, having got to know him a little, we are quite sure that none of the negative comments made by house movers in this book would ever be applied to him.

Thanks also to Ann Maurice for reading the manuscript and giving it such a strong endorsement. Ann Maurice presents a series of 'home staging' training courses geared toward homeowners, landlords, real estate agents and property investors both for business and personal use. For details about Ann Maurice's training courses visit **www.housedoctor.co.uk**.

Introduction

Moving house is one of the most stressful life events that we could ever undertake – yet the average person will undertake this task several times in their lifetime. Whether the move is an upgrade, a downsize, a first move or a 'December days' move, it will invariably involve coping with stress, change, upheaval and anxiety.

Psychology has a lot to offer the house mover, with tips and tools to help them through this difficult time. Yet, whilst there are many books out there covering the practical and legal elements of house moving, none have applied psychological insights to help the mover cope with the emotional side of the life changing transition they are embarking on. Upping Sticks aims to fill this gap by guiding you through the emotional roller coaster that is moving house. This book will help you decide whether the time is right to move; give you the psychological secrets to make your home irresistible to buyers; help you see through common ploys and tricks used by vendors; advise you how to cope with the kids during a move and even help you settle in once it's all done. Drawing on psychology research and theory, Upping Sticks will give you the tools to make your move run as smoothly as possible.

As well as its psychological underpinning, Upping Sticks draws heavily on the experiences of 100 house movers who kindly completed our research survey. We have used their stories to provide real life case studies, 'Our survey said' sections and to help us compile practical pointers, lists and 'Top Ten Tips' that allow a marriage of psychology with practical application. Everything from packing tips, to advice on coping with change is covered, making this book the ideal accompaniment for your house moving journey.

In addition, and for entertainment value as well as use, Upping Sticks features the unique People Watch sections which provide incisive personality profiles of the key players in your move. We help you identify and cope with different types of Vendor that you may encounter (such as 'Snakes', 'Sloths' and 'Pussy Cats'), different types of helpers who may help you shift your stuff (such as the 'Macho Helper', the 'Critic' and the 'Shirker') and even different types of neighbours you may encounter (e.g. 'The Gossip' and 'The ASBO Magnet').

All in all, Upping Sticks provides a unique and entertaining guide, packed with tips and psychological tools, to help you move house – and stay sane.

CHAPTER 1

So you've decided to move?

You feel like the walls are closing in on you, you have the neighbours from hell, you are aspiring to be upwardly mobile, you haven't enough space to display your ever growing collection of beermats...whatever the reason, you have decided that you need to move. You may not know where you want to go to or even where to start; you just know that you Gotta Get Out Of This Place (if it's the last thing you ever do). Read on to help you get your move moving.

Why do you want to move?

Moving house is not for the faint-hearted so it is important to understand why you want to move. Sometimes people want to move for the wrong reasons, just like some people have babies, cosmetic surgery or a whole tub of cookie dough ice cream in one sitting for the wrong reasons. Emotions are very hard to decipher – researchers have shown that one emotion pretty much feels like another and it is only our interpretation that helps us decide what we are feeling at a given time. Thus, we may feel lonely, depressed, stressed, anxious or otherwise unhappy with our lot. Instead of attributing this to other causes, we may look around at our peeling wallpaper, overflowing wardrobes and leaky guttering and conclude that a change of environment is just what the doctor ordered. Of course, some may instead look at their flabby, shell suited, toenail picking partner taking root on the sofa and conclude that a rather different change is what is needed, but that is another book entirely....

> **Our survey said...**
>
> The main reason that people in our research wanted to move was to upgrade to a large property. This accounted for a quarter of all respondents. Just under half that number stated their reason for moving as wanting to downgrade the size of their property. A further 10% claimed they were moving due to either their own or their partner's work relocation. Other reasons included to be nearer to their family, first time move away from the parental home or because of splitting from a partner.

So, let's look at some of the right reasons for moving – and some of the pitfalls to be wary of.

Downsizing

You are probably middle-aged (whatever that means these days) with children who have flown the nest and thus you no longer need a family sized house. Your grown-up kids probably still have their own room intact where they store their treasured possessions (dolls, teddy bears, collection of Playboy mags etc.) and they may even return a couple of times a year and sleep in their old beds. You are beginning to feel that your home is little more than a storage facility and occasional hostel. You begin to resent the inordinate council tax charges and heating bills you are paying for the privilege of looking after your offspring's collection of childhood mementos. And you positively yearn for a smaller place that is cheaper and easier to maintain.

Warning! Your kids will probably oppose any suggestion of your 'abandoning' their childhood home. They will have a lot of emotional baggage lingering amongst the soft toys and old school ties left behind that they will be in no hurry to dispose of. Expect intense psychological pressure to stay. Resist!

Upsizing

In this case you are probably part of a couple either expecting a baby (congratulations!) or already with a family that is fast outgrowing the space available. Perhaps you live in a flat (or apartment as estate agents seem to like calling them these days) or townhouse and are worried about schlepping a buggy or bags of nappies up the stairs. Or your current property is so tiny and cramped that you are seriously wondering how long it is reasonable to sleep a newborn in your sock drawer for without Social Services being informed (the answer, just in case you are still wondering, is about two months if the drawer is empty, and not at all if it's full). Or maybe you are just sick and tired of falling over bikes, scooters, roller blades, Lego bricks and assorted electronic toys that beep and sing 'The Wheels on the Bus' incessantly. Get thee over to the estate agents – what are you waiting for?

Warning! Move before you're pregnant if at all possible. Pregnancy is a stressful enough time when the number of decisions you need to make already grows in direct proportion to the size of the bump: type of buggy (three wheels, four? swivel wheels? convertible? high loading? integral car seat? colour?), type of cot (crib? cot-bed? bedside cot? one lock mechanism? adjustable mattress heights?), which baby sling (lumber support? shoulder support? integral soother holder? colour? material?)…need we go on? You really don't need the extra hassle of choosing a property, furnishing and decorating it at this time. If you have already left it too late, wait until baby is six months old and almost human-like before starting this major upheaval.

Flying the nest

You are young (ish), free, single – and solvent. You may have left home to study or work elsewhere, but financial constraints have placed you back firmly in mum and dad's fold for a few years now. Although you love the home cooked food, the laundry service and the fact that bills are never addressed to you, you are beginning to resent the intrusion and lack of independence; the questions asked about where you are going and who with; the lack of privacy for (potentially) hot dates and the general lack of coolness associated with a thirty-something still living at home. Time to take the plunge and dip a toe into the housing market.

Warning! Whilst Dad will probably have your bags packed after your first visit to the estate agent and a lodger installed after your second, Mum may well be devastated to lose you. She may encourage you to stay, constantly pointing out all the pitfalls of independent living (microwave meals for one, endless bills that *are* addressed to you and the shocking discovery that plates have to actually be loaded into the dishwasher and don't jump in there on their own). Don't weaken. Remind Mum that she won't so much be losing a daughter/son as gaining a spare room. And promise to visit regularly – but not too regularly (it defeats the object somewhat if you are home every evening for supper, trailing bags of washing).

December days den move

You are probably in your sixties, retired or approaching retirement and have managed to maintain the family home for years since your kids have flown the nest. You probably use the spare rooms to house grandchildren when they visit you and are reluctant to lose that facility. But, you are thinking ahead to when the stairs might become too difficult to climb and the garden too difficult to manage. It is time to think about moving to your December Days Den (referred to by some, rather less kindly, as your 'death nest').

"If you're moving to downsize later in life, do consider the value of good neighbours, and how you might feel confined in a smaller prop-

erty. Balance these factors and the need to dispose of excess furniture against the potential benefits." Bill, 58

Warning! This is a daunting decision because it means acknowledging the reluctant tumbling into the final instalment of your life. It means acknowledging that old age is around the corner and that you cannot really stretch the description of middle age to fit you for much longer. Nevertheless, there are many people who manage to embrace this life change with as much enthusiasm and positivity as previous life transitions, with plenty to look forward to and to occupy them. Hopefully, you will be one of them.

Work relocation move

You may be on your own or with a partner (or family), but need to relocate for work reasons. Perhaps it is your partner that needs to relocate for that promotion or amazing career prospect or perhaps your office is relocating or you have been transferred – whatever the reason, you are having to up sticks for professional reasons rather than personal. You may love your current house and think it perfect for your requirements, but needs must.

Warning! If you are half of a couple, there will almost certainly be some resentment from the party whose work is not the reason for the move. That person may have to find a new job in a new place and both of you will lose your current social and support networks. Moving to a new town or neighbourhood causes a great deal of upheaval and stress and an unwanted move will only add to the tension. Refer to the later section in this chapter on 'Trailing spouse conflict'.

The convenience move

You may be single or have a family and you may love your house. But the location is no longer suitable. Perhaps you want to be nearer a train route to get to work, nearer the shops or a park, or, more commonly, nearer the kids' school. You may even want to move in order to fall within an ever decreasing catchment area so as to get an elusive place in your preferred school. Whatever the reason, it is the all important location that is the key.

Warning! Whilst location is indeed of vital importance, be wary of thinking it is everything. Househunters desperate for a particular road or street are susceptible to falling into a range of traps designed to snare the unwary. You could end up paying too much for too little, end up with a property that fulfils none of your needs apart from location or you could be so blind to anything other than the postcode that you fail to notice glaring problems.

10/10 Top Ten signs that you are ready to move

1   On the bus journey to work, instead of being distracted by buxom passers-by in skimpy tops or 'Diet Coke Break' labourers at the local building site, you find yourself gazing longingly at houses with For Sale signs planted in their gardens.

2   When you visit your friends' homes, you find yourself mentally sizing up the rooms and wondering (hopefully not out loud), whether the hideous fireplace was there when they bought the property.

3   Your fantasies are more likely to include images of conservatories, open-plan kitchens and walk-in showers than anything even vaguely X-rated.

4   You go for a drive to a nice country pub and stop at 15 properties with For Sale signs on the way, miss last orders, stop at another 10 on the way back and end up buying some cans at the supermarket.

5   You pop out at lunchtime to buy a birthday card and come back with a handful of particulars from three estate agents in town.

6 You sigh a lot at home. When you can't shut an overstuffed cupboard, when you run out of places to move piles of papers to, when you notice another crack in the wall...all these things produce heavy sighs.

7 When browsing the shelves at your local newsagents you find yourself strangely drawn to the section groaning under the weight of home magazines.

8 You notice the eyes of your friends glazing over as you steer the conversation around once more to properties, mortgages and other equally exciting topics.

9 The local estate agent greets you by name when you pop in – again.

10 When you give visitors directions to your house, instead of using pubs and churches as landmarks, you use estate agent offices and particularly attractive houses as dominant features.

Where to move to?

Unless you are relocating for work purposes, or you are moving to a specific area to be near a school, you may have no idea about where to go. All you do know is that you want to move. The options are varied. Do you want to move from the city to the country, or from the country to town living? Perhaps you want to move abroad (see box below)? Or to suburbia or the commuter belt. Or maybe, you don't really care – you just want to find your dream home, irrespective of where it might be. Each of these options has its own merits and drawbacks.

City centre living

The great advantage of living in town centre developments is their proximity to everything a modern townie could require: shops, entertainment and work (assuming you work in town). Town centre dwelling, once the preserve of the poorest members of society who could not afford to move out to the suburbs, is now the domain of the affluent and upwardly mobile. Most city centres sport shiny new housing developments close to all amenities. If you live in the city you won't need a car (good job as easy parking is not a feature of city centre living), you won't be short of company and you will never be short of easy entertainment.

However, city centre living is not for those who dislike the hustle and bustle of busy town centres that never seem to sleep. Nor is it for those who yearn for peace and quiet, space or greenery. Sure, many developments have a few token trees or fountains and some are even located by canals, but these offer a rare and transient oasis of calm in a vast sea of turbulence.

Living in the country

Whilst you may get peace and tranquillity in the country (barring perhaps the early wake-up call of the local neighbourhood cockerel), you will probably lose the convenience factor. Shopping visits and entertainment often require advance planning of pilgrimage proportions. Cars are a must, and they'd better be off-roaders if you don't want to get stuck in mud or snow (or if you bump into the odd stray sheep). Even getting deliveries or workmen to visit can involve a level of negotiation akin to the plea bargaining of lawyers.

Country living is best suited to those who are fairly self-sufficient in terms of social needs (although your city dwelling friends will probably descend on you every weekend), work (good for teleworkers or those who work mainly from home) and entertainment (there may be a pub nearby but visits to multiplexes will be consigned to history). For more on moving to the country see *Out of Your Townie Mind* (also by White Ladder Press).

Market town compromise

Maybe you fancy country living but the thought of being sur-

"I thought we moved here to get away from the noise."

rounded by muddy fields as far as the eye can see is a bit too much 'country' for your liking. Moving to a market town could be an ideal compromise; you get the advantage of the country-side's bounty on your doorstep but with the added benefit of a bustling town for the convenience.

Market town living is best suited to those who don't like extremes; it's ideal for those who want their cake and want to eat it too. These places offer a good base from which to commute to the bigger metropolis, and also tend to have all the facilities that you need – albeit on a much smaller scale (don't expect the local M&S to stock its entire range of ready meals).

Moving to suburbia

Perhaps you want the best of both worlds: easy access to work, shops and entertainment but with the white picket fence cottage too. Your world is your proverbial oyster when it comes to choosing properties in the suburbs with your desires curbed only by your budget.

The problem with a decision to move to suburbia is the infinite choice and endless possibilities. How do you decide which suburb for a start? Too much choice can be paralysing and you could end up in a permanent state of inertia, always dreaming of a move that never happens. Drive around at different times of day (and night), look for transport links, shops, scenery and groups of ASBO seeking hoodies lurking on street corners. Be wary of the lure of unspoilt fields – some property developer has probably already got their beady eye on it. Talk to the locals and finally, check out websites such as Upyourstreet.com.

Moving abroad

Moving abroad is becoming more popular as people seek sun, sea, sangria (and other things beginning with 'S') as well as a more relaxed way of life. There are several of reasons for this type of move: the first is to retire to a place where the sun visits more than twice a year; the second is that the near continent is now actually within the commuter belt (you can – on a very good day – commute from France to Southern England in the time it takes to travel across London. Possibly.). Another reason is to take advantage of the current trend for teleworking whereby computer technology means that many jobs can be carried out away from the office, allowing you to work in your pyjamas in Paris or in your bikini in Bourdeaux (without people fleeing in terror).

A good source of information for those contemplating such a move is *Au Revoir Angleterre* (White Ladder Press).

Coping with major life change

"Change", opined Aristotle, "in all things is sweet". Maybe it is, but it can also be damned stressful. In fact, moving house is one of the most stressful life events we can be involved in. According to research, it comes in behind things such as bereavement, divorce and imprisonment in the list of the 43 most stressful life events that humans can experience (Holmes and Rahe, 1967).

Coping with any major life change is a challenge but some people are affected more than others. This is because we have different 'reaction-to-change' personalities, with some people embracing change and others resisting it for as long as they can. E.M.Rogers, in his landmark book *Diffusion of Innovations*, grouped people into five categories according to their 'reaction-to-change' personality.

Reaction-to-change personalities (based on Rogers, 2003)

Innovators: About 2.5% of the population accept new ideas quickly and are intrigued by new ways of doing things. They love change and are the first to get the latest phones, cameras or gadgets.

Early Adopters: About 13.5% of the population are also open to change but only after giving it very careful consideration. They are likely to be among the first to buy the new gadgets but only after being convinced of their value.

Early Majority: This is a significant section of the population (about a third) who will accept new ideas but only after seeing others (i.e. Innovators and Early Adopters) use them successfully.

Late Majority: This is another significant group, again covering about a third of the population. These people approach new ideas with scepticism and caution. They are very conservative and are likely to resist change for as long as they can. They usually need some kind of pressure (such as social pressure, orders from their boss etc.) before they will, for example, adopt new gadgets or technology.

Laggards: About 18% of the population are the last to adopt new ideas – if they ever do. They are suspicious of innovation and change and are only likely to succumb under extreme pressure from others.

So, if you are a Late Majority person or even a Laggard, coping with the major change of moving house will be even more of a challenge, especially if you never wanted to move in the first place, thank you very much. So, here are our Top Ten Tips for coping with change:

10/10 Top Ten Tips for coping with change

1   Identify your 'reaction-to-change' personality using the box above. Recognising that you find it difficult to cope with change is an important step to coping with the major life changing event of moving house.

2   Identify your worries. Even change embracers will have concerns about something as major as moving house. Identifying and writing down your concerns can be helpful and puts things in perspective. For example, many of your worries may be wrapped up in the actual moving process (Will my belongings arrive intact? Will it be easy to get my mail redirected?). Others are to do with the sheer volume of tasks that need to be completed (see Chapter 4 for more on this).

3   Talk to someone. Having someone to share your worries, fears and hopes with is invaluable and a healthy outlet. If you are part of a couple, you need to be on the same page. Even if you are not part of a couple, having a mate to bounce ideas and concerns off can help bring perspective to the process.

4   Anticipate change. Many people make the mistake of trying to

avoid change or pretending that the move won't be stressful – especially if they are excited about it. Even positive life events, such as getting married or promoted at work are stressful; and moving to your dream home is no exception. Don't let stress take you by surprise. Expect it and make allowances by either trying to plan a less stressful work environment at moving time, or building in some stress reducing time (e.g. visits to the gym or a health spa).

5   Expect to feel unsettled. Moving house is unsettling as is any venture into newness or the unknown. The lack of roots and feeling of personal territory can make us feel insecure and uncomfortable and these feelings can manifest themselves in many ways (such as being short-tempered or tearful). Make allowances for yourself and your partner, and ask others around you to be understanding too.

6   Know that there is an end. This is one life changing event that you know will end and that once the upheaval is over, you will feel settled and secure again. A good mantra to hang on to is 'this too will pass'.

7   Hang onto the familiar. When your world is a-changing, sticking to familiar routines, seeing familiar people and going to familiar places can be reassuring. Try to avoid changing your pub, library, supermarket, social life and route to work all at once.

8   Make time for change. Many people make the mistake of trying to absorb a house move into their normal routine or fit it in at the weekend. A couple of days off work can ensure you settle in and give you psychological security; there is nothing worse than trying to work knowing that your life is in turmoil at home.

9   Find the good. For people who resist change, it is easy to hang onto all the loss that goes with moving house: loss of good neighbours, of proximity to shops, of that room you adore etc. Instead, focus on the good aspects that the new house offers.

10 Finally, don't panic! Panicking can cause a narrowing of attention; this prevents you from thinking clearly and seeing the broader picture which in turn may make you less likely to keep things in perspective.

Dealing with tension and conflict

If you are buying a house with a partner, tension and conflict are almost inevitable at some point. However close you are as a couple, you are still two separate people with different ideas about what you want. And, of course, men and women can have very different ideas about what makes their perfect home. There are two main sources of house moving conflict and tension within a relationship.

Our survey said...

Over 40% of respondents to our survey claimed that they experienced either some or a lot of conflict with their partner in relation to some aspect of the move.

Trailing spouse conflict

A 'trailing spouse' is one who gives up their own job and/or social life in order to relocate with their 'significant other' who has been offered a new job. Traditionally, the trailing spouse has been female, but there are more and more men falling into the category now – adding new dimensions to the conflict. Tension for male or female trailing spouses arises from:

- **Loss of upward career mobility:** A recent study of trailing spouses found that accompanying spouses ended up in jobs not only with less pay but fewer benefits and less promotion opportunities than the one they were forced to leave behind. This is because they do not have the luxury of sitting it out, waiting for the perfect job to come along, as you do when you are still in employment.

- **Loss of social support networks:** Whilst both partners might experience this, it is worse for the trailing spouse who is likely to feel resentful at the loss. The work relocating partner has the chance to build up new support networks and friendships in his/her new job that are, initially, at least, denied the trailing spouse.

Both of these can lead to loss of self-identity, self-esteem and self-fulfilment. The trailing spouse feels less important than their partner – more of a supporting act than a main act – and can resent the huge upheaval required. The partner may be caught up in the excitement of the move and the new opportunities it brings, and fail adequately to consider the impact on the trailing spouse. They may also not want to acknowledge the sacrifices of their partner because that would bring with it guilt.

When the trailing spouse is male, the tension is compounded by the need to challenge culturally prescribed roles as he is forced to take the passenger seat and put his career second. It can be harder for the woman too, as attitudes towards relocating a family for her job can be less forgiving than when it is for the man's job. See Karen's story, below.

Karen, married and with three children, had already moved twice to be with her husband, Rob – once when he was transferred to a different branch and once when he was made redundant. A year ago she was offered a great promotional opportunity that was too good to miss. The whole family uprooted again, but this time, she says, attitudes she encountered were very different:

"My parents accused me of being selfish, putting my needs before those of my family. I was told by friends that our marriage would not survive as I was emasculating Rob. Everyone said I was being cruel to the kids and I felt like a heartless mother. We never got any of this hassle when we moved for Rob's work."

Deal with trailing spouse conflict by:

- Involving the trailing partner in as many decisions as possible. Avoid them feeling like a bit player in the move.

- Recognise and acknowledge the emotions involved: guilt on

the part of the relocating partner and resentment on the part of the trailer.

- Agree an exit strategy for the worst case scenario – preferably one that does not result in a Decree Absolute. For example, if the trailing partner hasn't found a decent job in a certain amount of time, is there any way out that can be arranged?

- Negotiate 'paybacks' for the disadvantaged partner to try and even up the weightings. This could mean the trailer gets the main vote in choice of house, or gets a room allocated for a home office or den.

Wish list conflict

This conflict occurs throughout the moving process and is tied up around diverging wants and desires. Common sources of dispute and discord are likely to be:

- **Location of property:** He wants to be near pubs, supermarkets and the local synthetic football pitch, she is more concerned about being in the 'right' neighbourhood with 'nice' people to wave at every morning.

- **Features of property:** He likes 'quirky' features such as sunken baths, cool outdoor decking for barbeques and mirrored bedroom ceilings. She is keen on huge kitchens, a safe garden for the kids to play in – and insists the mirrors must go.

- **Décor of property:** He will be perfectly happy with the décor of every house, even the lime green and orange living room; she will want to paper and paint them beyond recognition (especially the lime green and orange living room).

Avoid Wish List fracas by use of compromise and acceptance of differences. There is no point being frustrated at your discordant desires; accept them instead and look for areas of compromise. Whatever you do, avoid dragging a third party in to adjudicate, especially if it's your mum or best friend.

So, having decided to move, and having been prepared for all the attendant stresses and hassles, it's now time to put your house on the market...

References

Holmes T and Rahe R (1976) Social Readjustment Rating Scale. *Journal of Psychosomatic Research*. 1967, vol. II p. 214.

Rogers, E. M. (2003). *Diffusion of Innovations* (5th ed.). New York: Free Press.

CHAPTER 2

Selling your house – the art of persuasion

So, you are ready to take the plunge and put your much loved (or perhaps, in some instances, much-loathed-can't-wait-to-get-shot-of) home on the market. The process of selling your home necessitates as much psychological input as it does practical. As you meander through the murky minefield of excitable estate agents, muddy footed viewers (it seems to be an unwritten law that viewers must wade through a marsh swamp before entering your pristine home) and prospective buyers who are determined to screw you out of every last carpet, curtain and light fitting, you will need all your wits about you. Seller beware!

Getting your house ready to sell

First of all, get the idea of selling your 'house' out of your head. Using the psychological tricks employed by all good salespeople, you will realise that to shift your product, you must be marketing not so much a house or even a home, but preferably a *lifestyle*. Consumers choose one product over another for a whole range of reasons, only some of which have anything to do with its intrinsic qualities. We make purchasing choices because we want to be like the stars who endorse them, because we want their lifestyle, their looks (and their bank balances). We choose products that are 'cool' in the belief that we, by association, become cool too. We favour one brand over another because we believe it espouses our values and outlook in life.

So, if you want to sell your home, you want your viewer to desire your lifestyle. You want them to walk in and think, 'Yes, I could live like this'. This is not likely to happen if your property is cluttered, cramped, crowded and smelly (unless your viewer happens to be an eccentric old lady who keeps 53 stray cats in her kitchen and a pigeon coop in her bedroom). So, heed the Top Ten Tips on using psychology to get your house ready for the market:

10/10 Top Ten Tips for using psychology to make your home irresistible

1 Sort out any little DIY jobs that are obvious to the critical viewer. Where possible, this could involve hanging (tasteful) pictures to cover wall stains, using blu-tack to balance wobbly shelves and installing pot plants in strategic places (beware of overusing this tactic – houses filled with an entire Garden Centre of greenery can seem a tad excessive).

2 Make sure the entrance is a really strong feature. The so-called *primacy* and *recency effect* in psychology means that first and last impressions are the most important. Best get rid of that 'humorous' doormat with the rather unwelcoming message…

3 Along the same lines, ensure your house has 'kerb appeal'. This is the first and last view the prospective buyer will get – from their car as they arrive and leave. According to estate agent Jeffrey Normie, who has had two estate agent branches in Northwest Manchester for 26 years, "When I have shown viewers around a property and shaken their hands and said goodbye, I can guarantee that they will walk to their car, stop, turn back and face the house for a last look." The garden (if you have one) should be mowed and tidy (colourful flowers are a nice touch) and the exterior woodwork of your property might need a lick of fresh paint (but go for a neutral colour that fits in with the neighbourhood. Now is not the time for psychedelic pink).

4   De-clutter your home. Get rid of papers lying around, coats slung over banisters, piles of old magazines, clothes hung on door handles of wardrobes...oh, and all those crazy pot plants. You should be creating an oasis of calm and tranquillity, space and freedom. Clutter is, for most people, stressful and anxiety inducing...and suggests that the house is too small for all their things. But don't just stuff everything into drawers and cupboards – viewers will open these. If they are crammed full, they will worry that there won't be enough room for all their stuff (and they'd probably be right).

5   Hide any pets (and their traces). Oh, this is a tricky one, but pets really only appeal to like-minded people. Psychologically, we are attracted to those who are similar to ourselves; dog hairs, litter trays or hamsters running inanely round wheels do not foster attraction in those who do not find a hairy little furball appealing. And if the viewer finds you and your home unattractive, they will not crave your lifestyle. They may even be afraid or unnerved by your pet, especially if it is an overexcited Yorkshire terrier or a screeching parakeet. Play it safe and keep the house pet free (or get a goldfish instead).

6   Identify the time of day your house looks its best so that you can arrange viewings accordingly. This might be in the morning when the sun is filling the house with light, or the afternoon when the garden is full of the brightness of a summer's promise. Hopefully it will not be at three in the morning when the moon casts an eerie but romantic glow over your property.

7   Select an estate agent (if you are planning to use one). See box below.

8   Get rid of anything offensive or tasteless in the house. This includes 'girlie' posters in teenage boys' bedrooms (although tasteful arty prints in bachelor pads are probably OK), politically incorrect fridge

magnets and books entitled 'Rude Jokes from the Internet'. And you should definitely get rid of the singing fish that warbles 'don't worry, be happy' when you clap your hands.

9 If your house has furnishings or décor that are very 'you', be careful. The more neutral your décor, the better. Flamboyant colours, busy wallpaper, animal prints, Spanish themes to remind you of your favourite holiday…these are all bad ideas. A house that is too personal to you will make it harder for the prospective buyer to imagine stamping their own personality on. It also might make them throw up…

10 Get rid of odours. Banish smoking from the house, empty ashtrays and invest in natural fragrances like pot pourri or the smell of fresh bread (see later). Avoid air fresheners – they are so obvious and look as though you have something to hide (which you may well do…). Hint: a drop of vanilla extract in a hot oven will create a great smell (but might make you hungry – expect to put on half a stone before you sell your house).

Our survey said…

The most common thing that sellers in our research did to get their house ready for viewers was to tidy and clean it, with around 80% of respondents having done this. The next most common strategy was to remove things from sight (e.g. computers and other valuables such as jewellery; toys, washing, etc.) with over half claiming to have done this before a viewing. About a third of people followed time-honoured advice to create nice smells like baked bread or coffee to tempt buyers. A quarter depersonalised their house by, for example, removing photos or hobby paraphernalia. Other preparations included making sure the house was warm and cosy in winter and bright and airy in summer – and even filling the rooms with fresh flowers. Only 15% of our respondents felt the need to do any house improvements like installing double glazing.

"My boyfriend was trying to sell his house. It had been on the mar-

ket for about a year and no one ever came back after a visit. When I went round one day, I saw why. It was a mess. It looked like it had been burgled – stuff and junk everywhere. My boyfriend was adamant that viewers wouldn't be put off and that the house's potential would shine through. Eventually, I convinced him to tidy up and within six months, it was sold." Lucy, 23

"My fiancé and I went to view a house. It was great except when we went into the child's bedroom and saw a gerbil in a cage on the floor. I thought it would endear me to the vendors – and get us a better deal, perhaps – if I stroked and tickled this rodent. I stuck my finger in the cage and it promptly bit me. Not wanting to draw attention to my stupidity, I pretended all was fine and hid my bloody finger in my pocket the rest of the tour. We didn't buy the house." Jane, 26

Estate agents – the low down

How to select an agent: When choosing your estate agent, make sure that they are a member of the National Association of Estate Agents. This means that they should be reputable because they will have to comply with a code of conduct and ethics. According to estate agent Jeffrey Normie, "There is no substitute for personal recommendation when choosing an estate agent, but it is prudent when you visit their office for the first time to look out for this statement of membership. Other things to look out for include a statement that they are a member of The Ombudsman Scheme for Estate Agents – and, of course, that they have friendly and helpful staff."

What percentage to expect to pay: According to Jeffrey Normie, expect to pay between 1–1$\frac{1}{2}$% in fees to the agent.

Joint or sole rights: Jeffrey Normie points out that putting your house on with more than one agent is only beneficial when the agencies are in different catchment areas. Otherwise, he says, there is little point as most buyers tend to visit all the estate agents in the area, not just one.

What you can expect your Estate Agent to do (and not to do):
"A reputable estate agent should be working 100% on your behalf. They should be your champion to get the best price for your property. The first thing they do is value your property, or what is called a 'market appraisal'. They are obliged to give you their terms of business (for example, information about sole agency, commission, advertising, etc.) at that visit, or as soon after as possible."

Putting up a 'For Sale' sign or not?: Jeffrey Normie strongly recommends a 'For Sale' board outside your property. "I think the board is the best way of advertising your property, better than newspapers and the Internet. In my opinion, most buyers will live within a couple of miles of your property. I reckon that 90% of people move locally most of their lives, so the For Sale board is the most important way to market your home." Jeffrey explains that the most common reasons people give estate agents for not wanting a For Sale board are: (1) I don't want everyone to know my business/I don't want the neighbours to know'. "This", says Jeffrey, "is ridiculous. If you want to sell your home, you should want everyone to know." (2) 'Boards are ugly'. Jeffrey always reminds them that regulations exist now to make sure that they can't be bigger than a certain size, so, he maintains that this is not a good reason for refusing a board either.

According to Jeffrey there is a number of things that sellers can do to annoy estate agents. Here are his Top Ten:

1 Follow the agent round on viewings.

2 Refuse to have a 'For Sale' board (see above).

3 Think that they know more than the agent about selling houses.

4 Insist on putting it on the market at a higher price than it's worth.

5 Putting the property on the market just to test the waters and then taking it off thereby wasting everybody's time.

6 Being deceitful by taking it off the market and pursuing a sale privately with a buyer.

7 Leaving their house untidy.

8 Making access difficult for viewings.

9 Not returning phone messages from the agent.

10 When joint vendors disagree with each other about whether to accept an offer.

Whether you use an agent or not, you will have to agree a price at which to put your house on the market. Many sellers make the mistake of going for as high a price as possible, on the basis that they can always reduce it if no one bites. Big mistake. A house that is reduced is old news and will never recapture that initial flurry of interest. Besides, prospective buyers will assume you are desperate so might make even lower offers. You could end up having to accept a lower offer in the end by putting it on initially above market value. It is far better to price realistically to start with, or, take the property off the market for six months then start again.

Home improvements that add value

According to Jeffrey Normie, these are the home improvements that would add the most value to your house:

1 Decluttering.

2 Removing pet traces, especially dogs and dog hairs.

3 Neutral decorating (i.e. white, off-white, magnolia.)

4 A new kitchen or bathroom.

5 Tidying up the garden to give kerb appeal.

6 Ensuring the windows look good.

7 If you have the money, double glazing, loft conversions and a conservatory.

Now that your house is a tip-top, clutter free oasis of calm and tranquillity, you are ready to cope with the onslaught of viewers (assuming you haven't improved your home so much that you decide to stay). These potential buyers come in many forms: singletons, couples, families and sometimes even extended families with granny, Auntie Ethel and the nanny in tow. However varied their form, the viewer tends to have one of four personality profiles. Analysing their personality type will help you identify their weaknesses and give you something to work with (and give you something to distract you whilst they violate your home).

People Watch: the personality profile of the potential buyer

THE SNOOPER The first thing this viewer will want to know is why you are moving. This will be followed up by a barrage of queries of such tenacity that you will be wondering if your viewer is a distant cousin of Jeremy Paxman. They will want to know everything about you and, if you let your guard down, will tease out family secrets and hidden nuances within no time (see below). For example, they will question the history of any ornaments, thus establishing your holiday patterns over the last decade. They will probe you about every stain or blemish in your house, so woe betide you if your crockery throwing antics at your partner left a dent in the door. They will also open every cupboard and door (including the fridge and your undies draw) so any attempt to hide undesirable objects will fail miserably (tip: bury your Rampant Rabbit and Turkey Twizzlers in the garden).

"We had some really annoying viewers come round, and they kept asking us personal questions not connected to the house. For example, they asked about our job, our place of work, even asking which building we worked in. They asked us what our star signs were, tried to find out where my wife buys her clothes from, and

asked me what kind of films I enjoyed watching. We felt that they were trying to analyse our personality and this made us feel very uncomfortable". Mike, 52

Deal with The Snooper by indulging their need for knowledge. Pretend to give them juicy snippets of information, especially if you can use them to make it sound like you lead a glamorous life within an oh-so-glamorous neighbourhood....

THE CRITIC This viewer will pull your house to pieces. Not literally, of course, although you might feel like knocking the whole thing down and starting again by the time they have finished. They will criticise the décor, the furniture, the size of the rooms, the lighting, the lack of a second (or third, or fourth...) loo, the location of the cloakroom, the state of the garden...everything. They will act as if you are not there and

The Critic: *"Do you mean to say you've lived in this house for five years without a mixer tap?"*

wonder out loud who on earth could live like this. They will complain about the estate agent's description of the property and moan about how far away your house is from the shops/school (or how near it is to the railway line/motorway/airport). This viewer is a real joy.

Deal with The Critic by distancing yourself – literally if possible, or emotionally if not. If the estate agent is showing The Critic around, leave them to it. If you can't leave, try not to take it personally. It may well be a ploy to try and knock the price of the property down or they may just be very insensitive people. Get over it.

THE TIME WASTER They are not here to buy but just to have an afternoon out. Some people really are so sad that traipsing round other people's homes is their idea of fun. They like to see how others live and perhaps feel smug about their own home. You will identify the Time Waster by their suspicious lack of interest in your home. They won't be carrying the estate agent blurb like everyone else and they won't ask any sensible questions about access to shops or schools. Instead, they might make coy comparisons to their own home of which they will speak fondly.

Deal with the Time Waster by getting rid of them. Always make sure your viewer is a serious buyer by ensuring they have the means to buy (your estate agent should do this for you too). Ask them about their position in the housing chain, whether they have a property to sell, whether they have a mortgage sorted, etc. If they seem vague about such details they are probably wasting your time. Of course, if you are a sad, lonely person yourself, you might be quite happy to have such people round – in which case, offer them tea and get the biccies out. You might make new friends and go on house viewing outings together…

THE POKER PLAYER This viewer gives nothing away. They will manage to view your entire house without giving any indication as to their intentions. You will have no idea whether they love your property or hate it. The Poker Player is determined to play it cool so that they can feign disinterest and try to knock a few hundred quid off your home. They know that if they enthuse, the chances of nabbing that to-die-for lime oak corner unit as part of the deal are slim.

Dealing with the Poker Player is tricky since all sellers want feedback. Asking them outright what they think won't help, especially if they are good impression managers. Instead, use some psychology of emotion and lie detection. Watch out for discrepancies between what they say and how they act – for example, smiles that don't reach the eyes. Ask them indirect rather than direct questions; it is easy for the practiced Poker Player to adopt a neutral expression when giving a prepared neutral answer ('Are we interested? Oh, it's early days yet/lots more properties to see etc.') to a direct question. Asking a more indirect question such as 'Do you like the area?' might lower their guard as they are less likely to have a stock answer to draw upon.

To really get to the Poker Player's true feelings, watch their hands and feet for giveaway tells rather than their face – these body parts tend to give more clues about real feelings. For example, we tend to make less expressive gestures with our hands when we lie than when we tell the truth. Of course, they may think you a little strange if you talk to their feet all the time or stare obsessively at their hands (especially if they are clasped behind their back) – probably wise to have a partner or mate do the staring whilst you do the talking.

Coping with viewings

Viewings can be stressful for vendors (see 'Our survey said') who have to cope with strangers traipsing through their home, making unwelcome comments and asking difficult questions (such as, 'Is that damp on the wall?'). When showing your house, you have to learn the gentle art of impression management – which is all about presenting your home in the best possible light without actually lying. You have to be on your guard at all times so that the fine line between impression management and deception is never, ever crossed (well, hardly ever).

Our survey said...

Nearly half of respondents to our survey found the experience of having viewers wander around their home less than enjoyable. The emotions they experienced ranged from being 'uncomfortable' (34%), 'irritated' (one seller was particularly irritated by the viewer lifting the lids off their pots to see what they were having for dinner) and 'annoyed'. Interestingly, 12% actually enjoyed the experience. The remainder were totally unfazed by it all.

10/10 Top Ten Tips for dealing with viewings

1   Get pally with the viewer... The similarity effect means that the more like them you seem, the more they will think that a house that you were happy with will make them happy too (a form of social validation whereby we look to similar others to validate our views).

2   ...But don't get too pally with them. Imagine they are a customer and maintain a professional distance. If they wheedle their way into your affections and you make the mistake of thinking they are your mate, you are liable to let all kinds of things slip out. Don't do it!

3   Always sound upbeat and cheerful. Emotions and moods are highly infectious and spread like a particularly contagious social virus. If you are dour and miserable, they will soon catch your mood and will only be able to associate negative feelings with your property.

4   Don't talk too much. The less you say, the less likely you are to put your foot in it and reveal more than you intended about the dodgy neighbours, the temperamental heating system and the on-street parking difficulties. Answer questions but avoid volunteering information.

5 Do play it cool. It is OK to imply that you have others interested in your home – even if they are the first ones over the parapet this millennium. Humans desire things that they can't have and covet things that others find desirable. So, if your viewer is under the impression that people are clamouring to buy your property, they will be psychologically drawn to find it that much more desirable – the so-called scarcity principle.

6 Do keep small children out of the way. They can be brutally honest. Enough said.

7 Don't get your hopes up. Viewers are strange creatures (see People Watch earlier) and the really enthusiastic ones are often the ones you never see again. Who knows why – it is one of life's great mysteries akin to the Sock Black Hole in the washing machine. No one really knows why it happens or where they go. Accept it.

8 Resist the urge to get defensive about negative comments. It is best all round just to smile sweetly. Unless they criticise your kids. Then it's all out war.

9 Bake bread (grind fresh coffee, deck the place with fragrant flowers...). It's corny, but it works. Research shows that pleasant experiences evoke positive memories and smell is a very evocative sense. Your viewers will think wistfully about your house without directly linking their yearnings with your dough making abilities. Unless they are wheat intolerant, or have an allergy. In which case, they will probably never darken your doorstep again.

10 Give the viewer space. Don't hover. Prospective buyers often feel very uncomfortable in someone else's house and might be intimidated by having the owner glaring at them each time they open a cupboard.

Negotiating to sell

It pays to understand the psychology of negotiation and recognise that the best transactions are those in which the seller and buyer both believe they got the best deal. As seller, you give yourself poor bargaining power if you fall into the following traps:

- You are desperate to sell. Desperation clouds judgement. This means that you might accept a lower offer than is reasonable, or might be pressured into agreeing to a large reduction in price on the basis of relatively minor problems uncovered by the survey. Desperation is also an emotion easily detected by the buyer and they will realise that they have the upper hand in any bargaining strategies.

- You are too emotional or sentimental. Selling your home *is* an emotional experience, especially if you have many memories tied up with the property. Hearing prospective buyers slag off your poky sitting room (which to you, was a cosy space to breastfeed your babies), shambolic garden shrubbery (where memories of many a halcyon summer linger) or slightly lopsided bedroom furniture (lovingly crafted by your dear dad) is not easy. But it is crucial to stay detached so as not to lose valuable bargaining power.

By wising up on the essence of consumer psychology, you can utilise a few sales techniques to help your negotiating stance. The aim, of course, is not just to shift your product (your home), but to maximise your profit. Use the following strategies:

- **Allow room for bargaining:** Decide what price you want for your property, then add to it. This allows the buyer to 'knock you down' and feel they have got a bargain. Estate agent Jeffrey Normie reckons 5-10% above the valuation is generally about right although he stresses that this depends on the property.

- **Build in some concessions:** If you can't move on the asking price, build in some other ways that you can appear to compromise. Buyers want to feel they have negotiated well and won a good deal. Meet this psychological need by perhaps offering a 'decorating allowance' specifically to do up a room they hate, or offer to do repairs or essential work before they move in. Furniture and appliances can all, of course, be negotiated – remember that it is not always the goods themselves that are important, but the feeling of winning.

- **Keep 'em waiting:** Once an offer has been made (whatever it is), let the buyer stew for a while. This will create the impression that you are not desperate and maybe have a few other offers to consider. Remember that basic rule of human psychology – people want what they can't have, so maintain that *illusion of unavailability* for as long as possible.

- **Resolve easiest issues first:** By resolving, or perhaps even giving in with smaller conflicts, you have created a state of cognitive investment in your buyer's mind. They feel that they have invested so much psychologically with you, that it is hard for them to back out now.

- **Compromise:** If you make a concession, the *norm of reciprocity* means that they will feel psychologically obliged to return the favour.

- **Steer them towards small commitments:** Salespeople use this all the time. They get you to agree with 'little' statements, for example, that you like the product or that you need a house near a school. Humans have a need for *consistency* so it makes it much harder to say 'no' when we have already agreed that the product is perfect for us.

- **Know your customer:** More educated punters respond to a more reasoned argument whereas you should take a more emotional path with the less educated. For example, explaining that 'the current trend is for properties in this area to retain or increase their value' will appeal to the more educated – whilst waxing lyrical about how happy you have been in the house will appeal more to the less educated viewer.

- **Watch your body language:** Never appear defensive when talking about your property (not even when next door's dog charges through your garden, rips your washing line down and pees on your newly washed shirt). Maintain an open posture (arms uncrossed, relaxed stance, eye contact, etc.) even when faced with the most difficult of questions.

Seller's timeline

- Visit estate agent to arrange a viewing/valuation and to enquire about obtaining a home information pack (seller's pack). For further information about the seller's pack, visit **www.homein-formationpacks.gov.uk**

- Agree price and launch date.

- Get in touch with a solicitor but don't instruct them until you get a buyer.

- Get your house ready.

- Get an offer and accept it 'subject to contract'.

- Wait for survey results.

- Renegotiate offer if appropriate.

- Exchange contracts.

- Complete the sale.

So, having exercised your sales skills, it is now time to put the boot on the other foot, and become the viewer. It's time to get out there and find yourself a nice 'des res', the house of your dreams...

CHAPTER 3

Buying your dream home – without nightmares

And so, having sold your house, or at least with the process underway, it is time for you to find the house of your dreams. Now it's your turn to become the invader and to go poking around the bottom drawer and bathroom cabinet of someone else's beloved home. Of course, having armed you with all the tricks to employ in the previous chapter, it is worth reiterating that people will probably be using these and other tricks (although that is a word with such ugly connotations) to get you to buy their home.

A word of warning

Buying a house is a veritable emotional roller coaster ride but unlike its theme park counterpart, you never know when the peaks and troughs will end. Be prepared for severe mood swings, as you lurch from despair to ecstasy – and back again. One minute you find the perfect property and you put in an offer, but the next you find the offer rejected…..then you make a counter offer which is accepted (oh joy!) but then you find that the surveyor's report throws up problems…

Being owned by your emotions in this way means that the more rational part of you is overwhelmed and relegated to a dark and dusty corner of your brain. This may cause your judgement to be clouded and susceptible to emotional biases such as halo and horns effects; this simply means that one outstanding feature of the house can override all the negatives (halo effect) or the opposite whereby one bad feature can irrationally outweigh the positives (horns effect). The point is that rational decision making goes out the window as we become slaves to our emotional puppet master. This chapter will help you cling to some modicum of rationality.

Fasten your seatbelt and prepare for the ride.

Don't believe all you see

A good house seller and their estate agent can be like a magician and their faithful assistant: they may try to misdirect your attention with simple sleight of hand, amaze you with tricks to suggest their property is the house of your dreams, and may use illusions to make you see what they want you to see. Fortunately, they will stop short of sawing you in half (probably). Your job as potential buyer, is to see beyond the smoke and mirrors of the illusions presented to you.

Preparing for a visit

A trip to your potential dream property should not be taken lightly and preparations should be considered carefully. Where possible take someone with you (but don't take your entire family – see below); this has the benefit of giving you an ally against any possible attempts by the sellers and agent to intimidate you or outmanoeuvre you. Psychology tells us that it is easier for two people than one person to resist pressure e.g. if they are trying to pin you down as to whether or not you like the property/intend to put in an offer.

"We were showing our property to some viewers and they asked if they could bring some family members to a second viewing. They

turned up with seven extra people. It felt like we should be charging them an entry fee for the guided tour." James, 41

Having the extra person also enables you to slip into a 'good cop/bad cop' routine if necessary; for example, one of you might enthuse about the property to schmooze the owners, whilst the other is more critical and reticent. This can have the effect of keeping the owners sweet (so they like you and want you to buy their house) whilst ensuring that they know you're not pushovers.

Of course, another benefit of having a companion with you, is for safety reasons. If you have to go alone, make sure you tell somebody exactly where, and when, you are going. For further guidance on personal safety visit the Suzy Lamplugh Trust web-site (**http://www.suzylamplugh.org/home/history.shtml**)

On a more practical note, you need to go fully equipped: take the following items with you:

- Notepad and pen.

- Tape Measure.

- Estate agent's particulars.

- Furniture measurements (probably for a second visit).

- Room measurements from your current house (for comparison purposes).

- Digital camera: you will forget some of the finer features of the houses, especially if you are visiting several properties (but don't forget to ask permission).

Arriving at the property

"We turned up at a property in Stanley Road, were invited in and offered a cup of tea from the gentleman who owned the house which

we accepted gratefully. As we sat, we began to wonder when we could start the viewing. His wife came down and gave us a puzzled look, but it was only when other people started to arrive that we realised there was a family gathering taking place – and we suddenly realised that we were in the wrong house. Our property was in Stanley Avenue. The gentleman had thought we were some distant relatives, so it was very embarrassing all round. We made our apologies and beat a hasty retreat." Jacqui, 42

Be aware that the viewing should start before you even enter the property. Take a few moments to pause outside the house, and look around. Take a note of the condition of the front of the house, the front garden, even the state of the neighbours' properties. Get a general feel for the ambience of the area – does there appear to be evidence of children around (bear in mind the time of day at which you make your visit)? Is it a busy road that could mean noise pollution? Are there any 'sites' nearby that might attract a lot of traffic, such as a school, a church, even a football ground (see below)?

"We bought our house, knowing that it was around the corner from a local football team's home ground. This didn't bother us as the team in question was so low in the league tables that we couldn't imagine there being a problem with crowds of supporters. However, a few months after we moved in, the team was promoted, a feat that was repeated the following season. So, having gone from a lowly league position, we now found ourselves living around the corner from a Premiership team. Crowds of riotous supporters regularly flock past our house on a Saturday afternoon, and the noise gets quite unbearable at times – along with litter in our front garden. They also park across our driveway and block us in. Our only hope is to sell our house to some dedicated supporters". Clare, 31 and Richard, 32

"We found the perfect house which we viewed on a Sunday. The owners insisted that it was the only day we could view. Luckily, just before we put an offer in, we went to visit the street on a weekday and dis-

covered that trains thundered by at a hundred miles an hour behind a fence that backed on to all the houses". Lucy, 31

Fault finding

Once you're in the house, it's easy to get distracted by that airy open-plan living room, by the delicious aroma of newly baked bread wafting out of the Aga oven, or the inviting jacuzzi in the en suite bathroom. However, one of your principle aims is to find any faults that exist in your potential new home. You need to pursue this task with the single-minded determination of a heat seeking missile. Leave no room unexplored and no corner unvisited.

If, on your initial inspection, there appear to be no faults with the house, then don't leave until you have found some. Of course, the shrewd seller will present you with one or two minor blemishes just so you don't get too suspicious. Beware of these as they may be hiding even bigger problems.

It is definitely best to find the problems on your own, so, it may mean taking tools with you to pull up carpets and move furniture (no, just kidding). But seriously, you need to have your wits about you to spot the problems. Look for tactics such as being ushered into and out of a room too quickly, for example the estate agent saying 'so this is the family bathroom, nothing really out of the ordinary here, so we'll move on to the master bedroom...'. Key phrases such as 'nothing really out of the ordinary here' should set off warning klaxons in your head – this is your cue to go back into the room and comb every inch of it to find out what the sellers are trying to hide.

Seeing through the deceptive smoke

One way to get a more accurate picture is to ask the owner questions and make careful note of the answers. From a psychological point of view, most people don't like to lie, and so will choose careful phrases in response to your questions to cover things up. Watch out for the following:

Non-categorical answers

Q: *'Do you have problems with condensation/damp?'*
A: *'Nothing major really – just the usual you might expect.'*

Any answer that isn't categorical i.e. yes or no, should be treated with suspicion. By all means give the vendor a second bite of the cherry by asking the question in another way but if they still don't give a straight yes or no, start to worry. Also, deceptive answers tend to be vague so, in this example, it's difficult to know what 'you might expect' or 'nothing major really' actually means. Try to pin them down on specifics.

Vague answers

Q: *'What are your neighbours like?'*
A: *'Oh, they keep themselves to themselves.'*

Translated, this is likely to mean a) that they don't get on with them or b) that they know nothing about them and don't want to admit it in case either they or the said neighbours appear unfriendly. One way to get further clarification could be to ask something specific such as how often do you see them/talk to them etc. Any vague answer could confirm your fears about difficult neighbours.

"We asked one guy about the neighbours, and he started to say how nosy they were. He then proceeded to back-pedal by saying how good it was that they looked out for each other, especially when the local kids took it upon themselves to just let themselves in to the house..."
Jill, 34

Diplomat's diversion

Q: 'Does next door's dog ever bother you?'
A: 'Oh, he's a lovely animal – ever so friendly'.

This is an example of the 'Diplomat's diversion' (typically used by politicians) i.e. total evasion of the question. In fact, by answering an entirely different question they have demonstrated a clear desire to avoid the issue. This is a typical deceptive tactic. One way to try and get around it is to 'do a Paxman'; keep asking the same question until you get a straight answer. It is likely that a non-politician will crack well before the thirteenth attempt.

Half-truth tactic

Q: 'Do the neighbourhood kids cause you any problems?'
A: 'Well, they can get a bit high-spirited at Halloween.'

Beware the 'Half-truth tactic'. This is where they will happily give you a true answer, but not the whole truth. They will neglect to mention that the high spirits are not confined to October, nor even to any particular month of the year. One way to catch this, would be to ask a follow-up question along the lines of ... 'So, what are they like around Bonfire Night? New Year's? Christmas? Every day?'

Distraction

Q: 'Is your heating system efficient'?
A: 'Well, our new double glazing will ensure that you have no problems keeping the heat in.'

This is a classic example of using distraction to cover up problems. Be especially on your guard if they grab your arm and press your nose into the UPVC surround of the window to deter you from pursuing your heating queries. They are trying to accentuate the positive features whilst distracting from the negative. A good way to get around this ploy is to simply be persistent. Admire the finer points of the lead flashing but don't be distracted from your original line of questioning. Moreover, don't be embarrassed to keep asking. As humans we generally try to avoid conflict so asking repeated questions may make us feel uncomfortable. But, when you're planning to spend so much money, a little psychological discomfort pales into insignificance.

Seeing through the illusions

There are a variety of telltale signs that a master illusionist is at work. Their aim is obviously to cover up all of the less desirable features of the property. Some typical misdirections include the following:

Pictures in strange places

Excessive wall hangings and pictures, or those placed in somewhat bizarre locations (e.g. at unusual heights or too close to a window/door/each other) should raise an eyebrow. You will probably feel too awkward to peer behind the pictures or even to request to peek, but you could pass comment and gauge the reaction of the house owner. A nervous laugh, a weak/totally implausible explanation (e.g. 'We like lots of pictures' or 'Picture hanging is my hobby') or an attempt to usher you out of the picture festooned room as quickly as possible, should be regarded with suspicion. It is more than likely that they have been deployed with the specific aim of hiding unsightly blemishes, peeling wallpaper, damp patches or structural damage (see below).

"We went to one house and there was a 'Coldplay' poster on the wall in the hallway. We thought this was an odd place in a family home to have such a poster. When the vendors weren't looking, we peeled the poster back, and discovered a huge hole in the wall, stuffed with

paper. Don't be scared to look behind posters or move things if they seem to be in an odd position." Richard, 38

Creative placing of mats and furniture

A similar tactic employed by the devious home owner would be to use pieces of furniture and rugs to cover carpet stains or damage. Use your own distraction techniques by getting the person with you to create a diversion (for example, showing great interest in the collection of trophies on the shelf) which will allow you furtively to lift a footstool or raise a rug.

"We were in one property that we liked but thought that a wall unit was in a very strange position, close to the door. When the owner wasn't around, we shifted it. It was covering up a dog flap/door thing." Jake, 39

"Well, we just thought it looked... er... interesting there. It emphasises the... um... flatness of the ceiling."

Strange smells

Another ruse commonly employed by sellers is the overuse of smells to mask problems. Be suspicious if there are too many overpowering aromas in the house. You might expect one or two (especially if they've read our tips in Chapter 2), but a different smell in each room should cause you to raise an eyebrow or two (see below).

"One property we visited had an overpowering smell of air freshener about it. We found this stench very off-putting and wondered what it was trying to hide. We left as quickly as we could." Vicky, 22

Reluctance to demonstrate equipment

Also be on the look out for situations where the vendors are a little bit cagey about features of their house. On the face of it, the property might appear to be full of all the latest mod cons and safety features, but this may be just more 'smoke and mirrors' – you need to be able to look beneath the façade and get to the reality of the situation. Vendors may highlight certain aspects of the property but be reluctant to discuss them in further detail. For example, they can't quite locate the key for the fabulous patio door, or they make some excuse about not wanting to show you how their high tech burglar alarm works (see below). Don't be fooled by surface appearance.

"We were very impressed with the alarm system and sensors that we were shown, and never thought to ask for a demonstration. It was only when we moved in that we realised that the box on the front of the house was a dummy alarm box." Jasmine, 25

Once you have found out all there is to know about the house, you'll want to broaden your scrutiny to the immediate vicinity of the house. This is a process that will be overlooked at your peril. Having scrutinised the interior and its ground, you might think you have found your dream home, but it could quickly become the house of horrors if you later find out that it is built on the flood plain of a nearby river, that just around the corner is the meeting place where the local drug dealer holds court each evening, or that your street is on the parade route for the local majorette band who have marching rehearsals at 7:30am every Saturday morning.

Checking out the local area

There are several of useful sources that you should consult before making the final decision about purchasing a property:

- The Environment Agency – you don't want to be moving on to a potential flood plain (no matter how into water sports you are).

- Upyourstreet.com

- Local council website – e.g. check local planning permissions.

- Local newspapers.

- School league tables of the area.

- Police station (ask about crime figures for your street).

Our survey said...

Most people in our survey did seem to carry out at least some kind of check of the local area; only 14% of respondents in our research did not. Half our respondents visited the neighbourhood at different times of the day, for example at night, at school home time etc. 27% spoke to neighbours to get a feel of the area whilst the same number used the Internet to check out their local area.

People Watch: the potential seller

On your travels in search of a new home, you will find that the seller comes in a variety of forms. Watch out for the following:

The Sloths

This breed of seller appears far too laid back for their own good. They haven't bothered to tidy up the house, or even emptied the cat's litter tray. They also insist on carrying on with their day-to-day activities as if you're not there (which could be a tad embarrassing for you). In short, they have made no effort, believing that the house will sell itself without any input from them.

These people exhibit an 'external locus of control', which means that they believe factors such as fate or destiny, combined with the integral features of the house, have more of an impact than anything they can do. They are also likely to credit the viewer with the ability to spot the house's potential without having to make any effort themselves.

The way to deal with Sloths is to indulge them by inviting them to carry on with their lives and to pretend that you're not there (though you may want to draw the line at witnessing their more intimate moments – see below). Instead, take the initiative in the viewing, be prepared to make your own way around the house and not let them distract you from getting what you want out of the visit. Stick to your agenda and explore the kitchen even if they are sitting down for the family meal, examine the living room even if it means interrupting their viewing of Eastenders, or tiptoe around a bedroom even if one of their children is asleep.

"We went to visit a house, and were shown round by the owners. When it came to looking in the family bathroom, we were rather taken aback to find a young boy – presumably their son – sitting in the bathtub. He seemed as startled to see us as we were to see him. Needless to say we didn't linger too long in that room. We wondered afterwards if it was a clever distraction technique to prevent us from seeing things that were wrong with the bathroom."
Jane, 35

"In one house we visited, the owners clearly hadn't made any effort. There was underwear drying on the radiators, bins overflowing in the kitchen and the seller was really not interested in selling his house." Chmiel, 34

The Puppies

Too much attention can be a bad thing, and this, unfortunately, is what you'll get from Puppies. These are sellers who just won't leave you alone. They stalk you from room to room, always at your shoulder when you're trying to have a private word with your partner, seemingly unwilling to give you a moment to yourself to think.

These people exhibit an insecurity complex, continually worried about what you might be saying about their property, or about them, or what you might discover if left to your own devices. The most extreme of Puppies might be worried that you'll make off with some of their possessions.

Dealing with Puppies requires a firm, but loving hand. This will involve telling them that you need some time to yourself in which to consider their property. You can joke, if you think it appropriate, that you promise not to steal from them. However, if all else fails, you can throw them a stick to fetch – translated, this means sending them off on a useless errand, such as asking them to find the serial number for the water boiler.

The Pussycats

Just as real kitties are loving and adorable, so the Pussycat is charming, warm, and sweet. They will flatter you, compliment you, and generally be as nice as pie – in short, they are trying to be your best friend in order to get you to buy their property. They will tell you their illustrated life history using items around the house as cues, and will try to build a rapport with you. They appear cute on the outside, but beneath that fluffy exterior they are devious and manipulative, as they try to get you to feed them titbits of information about your intentions.

Pussycats are Machiavellian souls, motivated by a need to get what they want. Their interest in you, we're sorry to say, is fake, and whether you buy their property or not, don't expect to be on their Christmas card list.

Deal with the Pussycat by resisting the onslaught of their charm offensive. Be friendly but business-like, be cagey in the information that you release to them, and resist the psychological lure of the norm of reciprocity (e.g. they tell you their life story, which may or may not be true, and you have the need to disclose something about yourself in return).

The Snakes

There is always one visit that you'll go on where the property is occupied by somebody who, quite simply, makes your skin crawl. They are creepy, eccentric and generally make you feel very uncomfortable. The Snake might be a middle-aged man who lacks social skills and acceptable personal hygiene, an elderly spinster with 26 cats, three budgies and a selection of rodents in her kitchen, or a randy bloke who leers down your top at every opportunity and takes great pleasure in pointing out the mirrored ceiling in the bedroom.

"One property we visited smelled of wee and was disgusting and we couldn't wait to leave. Another house was so spotless, it was spooky e.g. the tins in the cupboards were lined up according to size and colour." Jo, 36

"Years ago, we viewed a house that was really dirty and the owners were scruffy, lazy, fat, dirty people. Though the house had potential, we couldn't ever live there as we would be worried about botched DIY/engrained dirt/infestations." Joshua, 34

> *"I visited a house on a Saturday morning and found two rather large men sitting on the sofa in nothing but their underpants, eating a fry-up and watching kids TV. It was very creepy and off-putting."* Naomi, 36

Snakes are considered rather odd by society in general, have very low social awareness and even lower self-monitoring abilities. This means that they are unable to recognise acceptable social behaviour and do not give enough consideration to the impact of their actions on others.

In general, we recommend you run away – surely no house is that good. Alternatively, you may just need to brazen out the situation. Try to be comfortable with the uncomfortable – sometimes different is not necessarily bad. At the very least, you may get a good house moving story out of it.

Whatever kind of person the seller appears to be, there are a number of useful questions you should be asking. These include the following:

10/10 **Top Ten questions to ask the seller**

1   Why are you selling and where are you moving to? (see below)

2   How long have you been here?

3   What are the neighbours like and have you had any disputes with them?

4   What's the worst thing about living here?

5   What's the best thing about living here?

6   Will the survey reveal anything of concern?

7   Is there a chain and are you looking to move quickly?

8   How flexible are you prepared to be over the price?

9   What kind of interest have you had in the property?

10 Is there anything about the property that might have an adverse effect on us such as County Court Judgements or credit rating problems? (see below)

"Something I would do for the future would be to check –before I signed the contract – to see if the current owners had any debts, as we were inundated with calls, and the mortgage company had a representative turn up at the door. This was in a decent area so it was a shock, and I'm thankful that the bailiffs didn't bang the door down wanting my things even though the old owners had 'done a runner to Spain'. Now I realise why they were happy for us to move as quickly as we could and I know now why they were going abroad."
Rayna, 34

"We moved out of our new house after finding out that the previous owners had left thousands of pounds of debt and mortgage arrears. This affected our credit rating; in fact we only found out when my husband applied for a new credit card and was refused."
Deborah, 34

Question 10 may be a little difficult to ask because it appears confrontational, however it needs to be asked as it has implications for your future credit rating. One way to diffuse any potentially awkward moments arising from this question is to say that you weren't necessarily referring to the present owners but were wondering about previous occupants.

Negotiating to buy

Once you have decided that you want the property, you are now into the critical stage of persuading the seller to give you the best possible deal. Keep in mind that almost everything is negotiable, including:

• The price

- Cost of any necessary building work/repairs

- Appliances e.g. dishwasher, washing machine

- Fixtures and furniture e.g. curtains, corner units

- Completion dates

The process of negotiation may make you feel uncomfortable because it may involve a degree of confrontation and possibly rejection. However, if you don't ask, you won't get, so be assertive and follow our guidelines.

Firstly, you need to make an offer – this means deciding whether to offer the asking price, below, or even above (in very buoyant markets). You should:

- Check prices of similar properties in the area if at all possible.

- Make note of how many similar properties are on the market.

- Take into account how long the property has been on the market.

- Find out how much interest the property has generated.

This will help give you an idea of how much to offer.

Make your opening offer, if possible, directly with the seller. This has the effect of not allowing them to hide behind an intermediary (the estate agent) and will allow you to appeal more directly to their reasonable nature (assuming they have one). Also, it will likely ensure that the negotiations are completed in one session, thus avoiding protracted discussions.

One-off house buying costs

- Stamp Duty: government tax on any property over £125,000 (at time of going to press)

- Mortgage Arrangement Fees charged by your lender to organise your mortgage

- Valuation and survey fees

- Seller's Pack – see **www.homeinformationpacks.gov.uk**

- Solicitor fees and local authority search to check out anything on the local authority records that may affect the property such as proposed road widening schemes

Other skills of negotiation

1 Choose your battleground. In all likelihood you will only have two options. The first will be to negotiate over the phone and the second will be to discuss terms face-to-face in the seller's home. Out of the two we recommend the second because it is easier to judge moods and feelings by observing body language and facial expression as well as listening to what they say. Where possible, steer the venue away from sitting at a table as this restricts your complete view of any body language 'leaks' that may be useful to you e.g. nervous jiggling of leg. Sitting in armchairs would be ideal.

2 Take someone with you. Even if they do not contribute much, they can have a reassuring presence and ensure that you don't feel ganged up upon. Sometimes you can get so involved in the proceedings that you might either gloss over something important that the vendor says or miss an opportunity to gain an advantage. A more dispassionate observer may notice such things and be able to alert you to them.

3 Always maintain a reasonable attitude even though you may be feeling frustrated. This means suppressing any negative emotions like anger or the desire to whack the vendor round the head with the TV remote control. Emotions are contagious and any negative feelings that you display may be mirrored by the vendor leading to a downward spiral in negotiations from which it is difficult to recover. Even if you do recover and buy the house, revenge may be wreaked upon you by the vendor you have annoyed (see below).

"Our buyer really pissed us off. He messed us about over everything and was aggressive and unpleasant. Even after we had agreed terms, he was still causing problems, screaming at the estate agent and threatening to pull out. My husband got so angry and stressed that he started plotting nasty things that we could do to the house that would only be discovered when it was too late... killing the plants in the garden, putting prawns in the curtains, spills on the carpet, giving the paintwork a bash every time we went past, losing all the instructions for everything, and forgetting the alarm code. Also, everything went with us when we left, even the loo rolls." Sam, 34

4 Never close any doors. This means taking care with your language: avoid *negative categoricals* such as 'definitely not' or 'no way Jose'. These show no willingness to compromise; whilst you may have already decided that the option is a no-no, it is best to couch it in softer terms such as 'I'm not too keen on that idea' as this avoids the vendor getting the feeling that you are not prepared to give even a little.

5 Always actively listen to what the vendor is saying. Avoid using the time when they are speaking as rehearsal time for working out what you will say next. Effective communication is a two-way process and the other person will be subconsciously looking for cues that you are indeed listening. Absence of these cues will suggest to them that you are not taking them seriously. A good way to show that you are listening is to use reflection by feeding back to them what they have said to show that you understand e.g. 'so what you are suggesting is...'

6 Avoid putting all your cards on the table before you need to. For example, don't let them know how much you can really afford until the very last minute. Honesty is not necessarily the best policy during such negotiations, even if it is your normal modus operandi.

7 Don't make an insultingly low offer. You may be tempted to try your luck by putting in a ridiculously low bid just in case they are so desperate to move that they accept it. This very rarely has any effect other than to aggravate the vendor and suggest that you are not treating them with respect. Make a realistic offer to bolster your credibility as a serious buyer.

8 Discuss the state that you expect the house to be left in. Don't assume that they will clean up and take all their possessions with them (see below).

"The previous owners had moved to a family property in Ireland and had only taken with them what they could fit in the car. The dishes were left on the draining board and much of the furniture, as well as food, cutlery, crockery and some personal possessions, were all left behind. Additionally, they had left a note apologising for not hoovering the carpets, explaining that their vacuum cleaner was broken – the dust was so thick it left clouds when you walked up the stairs." Claire, 27

"When I moved in to the house (which was being sold by the son of the occupant who had recently died), the house still had all her belongings in it. The washing machine was even still full of her washing. When I asked him to come and remove it, he said that they were included in the price of the house. I had just spent two weeks emptying my own house in order to move – this I found most stressful and disrespectful of his deceased mother." Demi, 34

9 Finally, be assertive. You will have a goal in mind that you want to reach and getting there won't be easy if you are too passive or aggressive. An assertive approach would be to put your ideas, wishes, desires and general message across in such a way that the vendor is quite clear about what it is that you want but is not offended in any way by the manner in which you express yourself. So for example, avoid raising your voice, banging the table, sulking, finger pointing and defensive postures. Instead, keep an even upbeat tone, maintain open body posture (e.g. arms unfolded) and good eye contact whilst sticking to your message.

However, be aware that you may have to use the above negotiation tactics with a third party who may or may not be totally honest with you. The job of the estate agent, let's not forget, is to get the highest price for the seller. It is entirely feasible that a less scrupulous agent will play one side off against the other and may even tell you that the offer has not been accepted without having mentioned it to the seller. You will either need to accept this risk, or try to make direct contact with the seller.

Once the dialogue gets going it is likely that there will be one of two outcomes: accept or reject. If your offer is accepted, your solicitor will set the legal processes rolling (the conveyancing, in legal parlance). If it's rejected, you have to decide whether to up your offer or walk.

10/10 **Top Ten Tips on how to know when you have found the house of your dreams**

It could be The One if...

1   You can, without any effort at all, visualise your possessions in each of the rooms.

2   You can look at the garden, and see yourself relaxing on a sunny day – whether it's soaking up the sun's rays, sipping a Pimms under a sunshade, or pottering about with a trowel in one hand and your watering can in the other.

3   Your children have already started to make friends with the kids from next door.

4   You are already starting to plan a colour scheme for each of the rooms.

5   You start mentally planning dinner parties in the wonderful open-plan kitchen/dining area.

6 You keep driving past the property to peep.

7 You worry about whether the current owners are looking after the place.

8 You start working out how long it will take you to get to work.

9 You start imagining the convenience of nipping to the local super-market on your way home from work.

10 You get a tingly feeling in your tummy whenever you think about the house.

CHAPTER 4

Neither here nor there

So, you've sold your house and now the waiting begins. If you're lucky, you will be able to time the handover of keys to your old house with taking ownership of your new property. If you are less lucky, there will be a gap between the date your buyers want you out, and the date you can take possession of your new place. And, if you're really unlucky, you won't even have found a new home yet. This chapter will help you through that uncomfortable stage of being neither here nor there.

The smooth transfer

If the transfer is seamless, the waiting game won't seem quite so drawn out. It will still be a tense time as you pray that nothing goes wrong whilst having to cope with the prospect of packing up and settling into a new home – which may need furnishing. Where possible, minimise the tasks involved; obviously, packing up takes priority so if you can put off choosing bedroom furniture or new patio doors until you are firmly ensconced in your new home, then do so. Just make sure that the essentials are in place, such as having something to sleep on.

On the other hand, moving to a property without niceties like curtains and dishwashers can be very unsettling and add stress for some people rather than decrease it. If this is you and the stress of being without outweighs the stress of all those shopping choices, then go ahead and do what you need to do. Even so, you shouldn't expect everything to be perfect the day you move in; just keep your mind focussed on the long term end goal (of your dream home) rather than any more transient shortcomings.

It really is a good idea, especially if you are moving locally, to arrange a few days grace after you take possession of your new home before handing over the keys to your old one. This will allow you to spread the move out a little, which is very handy if you are moving everything yourself (see Chapter 5). It also allows you to retrieve forgotten items or absorb any last minute delays that can be disastrous if everything is to happen the same day (see below).

"I thought I was being really clever arranging to hand over the keys for my rented property on the same day I was taking possession of my first home. Unfortunately, there was a delay of one day in my getting the keys and I was forced to move all my stuff out of my old flat, dump it in a sympathetic friend's house and then move the whole lot all over again the next morning. It took me two days of shifting boxes instead of one and was awful. I wish that I had allowed a few days overlap to prepare for contingencies." Abigail, 28.

The delayed transfer

If you simply have to be out of your home before your new one is available or ready, then you will probably need to rent somewhere to tide you over. Of course, if you have generous friends with very large homes, you might beg a stay over for a few nights, but that still leaves you with the problem of storing all your belongings.

Psychologically, this stage can be very stressful, as you really are neither here nor there. A long term rental of about a year can work, for example, if you are renovating your new home, but moving into temporary accommodation for up to six months can be deeply unsettling.

Exchange and completion explained

Once a sale is agreed, two identical contracts are drawn up and signed by seller and buyer. The solicitors representing the buyer and seller 'exchange' the contracts at which point the agreement to buy and sell is legally binding. There's no turning back. A deposit is paid at this stage too. A date for 'completion' is also agreed, which is the date when the keys are given to the buyer in exchange for the payment for the house.

So many things to do

This twilight zone when you are neither here nor there is a veritable hive of frenzied activity as it is essential to start preparing for the Big Move. Here are some Top Tips to help you through this phase.

4-6 weeks before moving day

- Start eating your way through your food. The less food that is left, the less there is to move. Start emptying the freezer, store cupboards and fridge. The closer you get to moving day, the more inventive you may have to be with this: it's amazing what you can conjure up with a tin of tuna, a box of cornflakes and a packet of breadsticks.

- Book a professional moving firm if you plan to use one. Get various quotes – this will usually involve them visiting your existing property to see how much stuff you've got. Find out what they will and won't do for their fee. For example, some will pack stuff, others expect you to do everything. Some provide crates and boxes, others charge you per box. Don't forget to show them your attic, shed, secret under floor compartments etc.

- Organise change of address details. Register to have your post transferred at the Post Office (it will cost you). Contact everyone who has ever written to you with change of address slips. Make sure that important contacts like bank and medical records are kept informed.

- Organise your utilities so that you are disconnected from your old address and reconnected at the right times.

- Get rid of the clutter. Car boot sales are great for this whilst charity shops will welcome bin bags of (good quality) junk. Be ruthless!

- Check out your entitlement for leave at work; many organisations allow special leave for moving house.

Packing tips

- Obviously, you will need all the accoutrements a house mover requires. This means sturdy boxes, packing tape, bubble wrap and newspapers. You can obtain some or all of this from the removal firm, although you may have to pay extra for them. Alternatively, the catalogue shop Argos now provides home moving kits (consisting of bubble wrap, crockery and glassware boxes, wardrobe boxes, tea chests, packing tape, marker pens and different sized boxes) which are ideal if you are not using a professional firm.

- Start packing the items you are less likely to need during the ensuing weeks. So, if you are moving in winter, you can safely pack summer clothes, summer toys, barbecue sets etc. A summer move is slightly less certain as you can never be sure that you won't need the sweaters and wellies. You should be pretty safe packing Christmas decorations away in June, however. Other items that can be packed early include pictures, ornaments, storage items (e.g. that 12 pack of loo roll) and kitchen gadgets that you rarely use (breadmaker, juicer, sandwich maker etc.). Even though this means going against standard wisdom of packing a room at a time.

- Label each box clearly as to what is in it (e.g. 'kids' summer clothes' or 'stuff from the under-the-stairs-cupboard'). This will help you find stuff that you've packed but that you will invariably desperately need. Also write on each box where it is going in the new home (i.e. which room). Don't write 'Stacey's room' as the movers will not know which room is Stacey's. Instead, write 'upstairs, front box room'. Indicate on boxes if they are fragile, if they should be kept upright or if there are any other special requirements (such as if you want it loading last so you can unpack it first).

"Darling, do you think we're going to need the fish kettle in the first few weeks?"

- Wrap glassware and crockery in bubble wrap rather than newspaper to save washing at the other end.

- Number your boxes and keep a list of what is in each numbered box. This way you will quickly be able to see at the other end if all your boxes are present and correct (and if one is missing, what it contains).

Our survey said...

Over half of the respondents in our survey used a professional firm to help them with their move. 40% made use of friends and family instead whilst 6% managed the whole move on their own.

DIY or professional mover?

The advantages of a professional firm are that they will do the job quickly, safely (you won't injure your back schlepping the bed out) and, well, professionally. They should be fully insured for any loss or damage and should also be able to supply all the kit you need (boxes etc.) although this may incur extra costs. A good firm uses clean personnel who put mats down to prevent dirty feet on pristine carpets and who don't demand cups of tea every five minutes.

The main disadvantage, of course, is the cost. Costs vary considerably according to the level of service you require (e.g. it costs less if you pack up your own crockery or supply your own boxes), and the distance you are travelling, but certainly runs into the hundreds. Some movers don't like the idea of unfamiliar men marauding through their property, or the thought of all your stuff disappearing into a van and being driven off by strangers.

The alternative, then, is to do it yourself. This is sensible if you don't have a lot of stuff to move (perhaps from a bedsit or studio flat) or you have a host of well built friends who just love the opportunity to flex their muscles and do a bit of weight training. However, you may not be insured for loss or damage and you and your mates run the risk of injury. The time and stress involved in DIY moving can be enormous and it can take several journeys (unless you rent a van of some sort).

However you move, a good tip is not to arrange to move on a Friday. Any problems that you encounter (for example, money transfer delays) may have to wait until the Monday to be resolved. You could end up with all your stuff in a removal lorry and no place to go. Also, if you are moving a long distance that involves motorway travel be aware that roads are hell on earth on Friday afternoons; far better to arrange a mid-week move where possible. If you are moving to a major city try to find out if there are any major events occurring, such as pop concerts, football matches or carnivals which could hinder your transit.

Time management

One of the reasons that moving house can be so stressful is the sheer number of jobs and tasks that need to be done – and the mother of all deadlines to meet. This section, then, is about using time management skills to get organised and prioritise your load so that the move and its run-up is as stress free as possible.

If there is one time management tip to swear by (rather than swear at), it's 'make lists'. Lots of them. Lists of things to do and things to buy. Lists of things to ask your solicitor. Lists of things to ask your mortgage lender. Even lists of the lists you've made (maybe we're getting a little carried away now). Lists are essential tools for the organised, time managing house mover. Take a note pad, or even better a ring binder (so you can add bits to it) and make different sections such as 'Two months before move', 'Day before move', 'Stuff for the new house' etc. When you've done a task, tick it off the list.

The next stage is to go through the list and allocate the tasks to appropriate people. This can involve more lists so, for example, you may identify several jobs for your partner and three for your teenage son. Make a new page with a list of tasks for each of them and include a completion date against each item.

Now, you will need to prioritise the jobs, probably by date order. The computer can help with this, so that you can move items about and create a time span of what needs to be done when (and by whom).

Other top time management tips with respect to moving house include:

- **Build in time for setbacks:** Allow time for interruptions and distractions. Plan only three-quarters of your available time; use the remaining unplanned time to provide the flexibility to handle interruptions and the unplanned 'emergency'.

- **Schedule tasks around your 'optimal circadian pattern':** This simply means knowing which time of the day is best for you in terms of particular tasks. Whether you are a 'night owl' or 'morning lark' try and work your tasks in accordingly.

- **Don't procrastinate:** If you have planned the run-up to your move well, you will know what needs doing when. Try and overcome the natural urge to put off unwelcome or dull tasks by employing a good old-fashioned reward system so that ticking three things on the list earns you a small treat (or why not a big treat?).

Shedding the past – how to say goodbye to your old life

Some people sail through this transition period without a backwards glance. They look forward, are enthusiastic and can't wait to start their new life. Most of us, however, experience at least a twinge of ambivalence about the move and some positively wallow in energy sapping pools of nostalgia for the life they are leaving behind.

Generally, how you cope with change will be the strongest influence on your ability to let go of the past (see Chapter 1). However, unless you have been deeply unhappy in your old home, the chances are that even the most ardent change embracer will suffer pangs of nostalgia as the move draws near. Here are some of the most common reasons to feel nostalgic – and how to make the goodbyes easier.

Neighbours

For those people fortunate enough to enjoy good friendships with the neighbours, leaving them behind can be a wrench. Good neighbours offer security, safety and familiarity, and you are saying goodbye to all that as much as to a few pals. Agreeing to 'stay in touch' only meets your 'affiliation needs' (i.e. your need for friendship) and not all those other things that having that safety net around you can represent. So, yes, you can still have summer barbeques together and drinks at Christmas. But good neighbours are more than that – they are somewhere to leave your spare keys, to borrow sugar from, to check your house while you are away, even to leave your kids with whilst you run an errand. The psychological effect of the loss of all this should not be underestimated.

However, saying goodbye to it all is easier if you stay positive. You can build a new safety net with your neighbours in your new property. Most homes have a potential for up to 10 sets of 'neighbours' so there is every chance that in time, you will build up a similar (or better) rapport with at least some of them.

The house

However much we want to move, we still become attached to the bricks and mortar of our own territory. The house might be too small, but how you love the view from the front window. It might be too far from your new place of work, but how you will miss the cosy conservatory. The little hideaways, the comfy study, the sitting room that catches the morning sun... all these can seem even more appealing when we know we have limited time to enjoy them. It is basic human psychology to take for granted what is easily and constantly available – and to crave and covet what we can't have (this is the basis of many 'offer ends soon' sales techniques that rely on our desire to want things of very limited availability).

So, being aware of this can make all the difference. Remind yourself how the appeal of your old house can rise due to the 'unavailablity' factor. You will soon have plenty to enjoy in your lovely new home, and without all the clutter.

The neighbourhood

It is not just the house or neighbours that can pull at the heart-strings at this time. Leaving the familiarity of the neighbour-hood and its surroundings can be just as hard. The local park, the convenient corner shop, the friendly pub, the quiet ambi-ence – all this can be hard to say goodbye to without some gen-uine pangs of nostalgia.

Overcome this by visiting your new place and checking out the surroundings (check out upyourstreet.com too). You are bound to find features of equal if not better appeal; perhaps a nicer park, a better stocked shop etc.

Memories

Ahh, the big one. These are the hardest things of all to say good-bye to. We all probably have the most sentimental and impor-tant memories of all tied up within our home. Memories of the kids growing up, playing in the paddling pool on a hot day in the garden, or building dens in the lounge. Memories of rela-tives, perhaps, now long gone, of grandpa sitting on his favourite sofa in the corner or of grandma adjusting her hat in the hallway mirror.

Although memories are intimately bound with the surroundings, they do, of course, exist most strongly within us. So, be reassured that you can take them with you, along with your furniture and clutter. It is a nice idea to take photos, however, of your favourite areas, just to remind yourself when your memories go a little fuzzy at the edges.

So, having shed the past, it's now time to look to the future because before you know it, the much anticipated moving day will be upon you...

CHAPTER 5

Getting ready for moving day

So, the big day is drawing near, you've said goodbye to your old life, and are ready to embark on the next stage of your moving experience (and it *can* reduce you to tears). This chapter will guide you smoothly through the hilly terrain of finally upping sticks and moving on. From your last minute to-do list, to Top Tips for surviving moving day, a smooth journey is (almost) guaranteed – and where it's not, we'll even help you deal with common problems encountered on moving day.

In the week before you move, there are many things to do. Let's start with the last minute packing...

Your last minute packing and to-do list

Inevitably, there will be items that cannot be packed, and jobs that cannot be done, until moving day or just before – accept it. Here are some last minute jobs that need to be done on moving day:

1 Make sure that you have arranged for final meter readings for electricity, gas and water – and ensure someone stays behind to facilitate this if you have to leave before the utilities person has arrived.

2 Don't leave the defrosting of the fridge until moving day – this should be done a day or two beforehand.

3 Put out the rubbish – leave the place as you would expect to find your new home. A little courtesy for the new tenants costs nothing – you never know when you might run into these people: it's a small world. It'll make you feel good about yourself too.

4 As previously mentioned (in Chapter 4) have an inventory of roughly what each numbered box contains, so if disaster should strike, and one of the boxes should go missing, you know what you have lost and what needs to be replaced. This will help with any insurance claims. It also has the psychological advantage of making you feel more in control of the move.

5 Make sure deliveries are cancelled e.g. milk, newspapers and the like.

6 Make sure any borrowed items are returned – no point schlepping any more stuff with you than you have to. So, return library books, next-door's lawnmower and DVDs to your mates.

7 Ensure your equipment is fully charged e.g. mobile phones, iPods and digital camera/video (see below).

Moving day survival kit

Pack yourself a 'survival kit'. This will be taken in the car with you when you leave your old home, and will include essentials to keep you going for the first 24 hours in your new home without having to unpack boxes and crates to find things. This kit is not only of practical benefit but of psychological benefit too – knowing that your basic comforts are available to you when all around you is in disarray.

This should include:

- A kettle, tea, coffee, sugar, and some long life milk.

- Cutlery & crockery – tea spoons (plastics will be best – no washing up), a breakfast bowl or two (depending on your numbers).

- Comfort food – biscuits (chocolate Hobnobs get our vote) to keep up your spirits when you start to flag, breakfast cereal for the morning after the day before.

- Any medication that might be needed – asthma meds, antihistamines, a pack of Anadin to cope with the headaches of the day.

- Lightbulbs – don't expect the seller to leave them behind. *"Researchers have found that it is the seemingly minor niggles that can really turn moving into a nightmare. Problems such as arriving at a new home and being unable to find the kettle and teabags whilst unpacking or not being able to turn on the lights because the previous occupants have taken all the lightbulbs with them"* (Daily Mail, July 9th, 2005).

- Toilet roll – enough said.

- Toiletries – toothpaste and brush, soap, make-up remover and the like.

- Distracting material – to allow you to escape for a few minutes, every now and then, the trials and tribulations of moving day. This could be your favourite magazine, a good book, a newspaper, a book of your favourite crossword/sudoku puzzles.

- A change of clothes – it can be a dirty job all this unpacking, so after the first push on unpacking, you'll need a bath/shower and a clean change of clothes to restore your humanity (don't forget to include a towel).

- Precious photos – this will allow you to quickly personalise your new home. It will rapidly push up the comfort feeling you have for your new place.

- Bedding – duvets, bed linen, something to sleep in, to facilitate a good night's sleep when you suddenly run out of steam.

- Essential items for communication – you'll need your mobile phone nearby to combat the psychological feeling of isolation as you move from one location to another, and don't forget chargers for your phone and rechargeable batteries.

- Other comfort items – such as a portable CD player to blast out your favourite inspirational tunes as you plough into moving day, or iPods if you're moving on your own and wanting a more solitary experience.

If it can go wrong...

It will. Here are some of the most common things that might go wrong on moving day, and how you can cope with them.

Removal men don't turn up

Fortunately, this rarely happens. If you are using a professional company, you will have letters confirming your removal date. It is worth checking these letters at least twice. It is a surprising fact that we don't always see what is there, but instead we see what we want to see. If we have it in our mind that an event will take place on a certain day, we just assume that the date on the letter is the right date. Check that the day and the date tally – so if the letter says 'see you on Friday 23rd', and your moving date is actually Thursday 23rd, you need to verify with the company that they will be coming on the right day. This may sound obvious, but there is a good amount of psychology behind why we make such basic errors.

If it does still happen that your removal company doesn't turn up (after all, people get ill, accidents happen – see below), and speaking to them does not lead to an immediate solution, you need a disaster recovery plan. The first thing to do is to inform all parties involved – your solicitor, your buyers – which will give you some modicum of control over the situation.

Remember that even the greatest disasters are resolvable. It may seem like your world is crumbling around you, but these things have probably happened before and will again. Try to keep the situation in perspective. Do not assume that the whole world is out to get you and that you should shoulder the entire burden alone. Let other people help. If you are reasonable about things, people's inclination to help will naturally emerge. The bottom line is that you shouldn't be afraid to ask for help.

"We were moving house on a cold winter's day, and it started to snow. This was OK, because the removal men put down some matting in the house so that they didn't tread all the slush inside. Unfortunately, the matting didn't extend up the garden path, and one of the men slipped and fell howling to the ground. He was in a great deal of pain and we tried to be sympathetic whilst worrying about our tight moving deadline. However, he really was injured and an ambulance had to be called. One of his mates went with him in the ambulance and we had to feed the other one cups of tea and biscuits. It later transpired that the poor bloke had broken his leg. We missed our moving day deadline, but at least we weren't liable as their insurance covered his injury. It did cause a lot of knock-on effects, and the people moving in to our house had to delay by a day too. Our advice? If it snows, be sure to salt your path." Lisa, 36 & David, 38

The keys to your new house aren't handed over on time

This could be for a variety of reasons, such as your money hasn't been transferred, or there has been a technical problem (see below). This kind of thing is likely to induce a great deal of psychological discomfort because we all need a sense of belonging. At this stage you will have left your old property, and now you have nowhere to go. This will evoke feelings of insecurity and displacement. Humans are territorial creatures, which is why people have their favourite armchair, or familiar place at the table. Our cave dwelling ancestors have a lot to answer for, as it is in them that we probably find the roots of our modern need for a place to call our own. The prehistoric world was a dangerous place to be: they had to contend with predators out to make them the main meal of the day, the uncertainty of finding food, and many other worries to boot. The sanctuary of their own cave was not a luxury but a necessity – it gave them somewhere to rest, to plan, to recover from any injury, and to hide. Fast forward two million years, and deep down, we may still have this deep rooted need for such a respite.

Any delay in picking up the keys is likely to be a temporary one, but our deep rooted fears are likely to blow it out of all proportion. We can cope with this by reminding ourselves that we're simply slaves to our ancestral drives. On a practical level, make sure that your solicitor and bank are on the case. On a psychological level, you may need to establish a temporary cave, such as the home of a friend or relative (or in extreme cases, a local hotel).

"It was house moving day, everything was packed, and the removal men had set off. I toddled off cheerily to my estate agent to collect the keys only to find that she was off sick and had the keys with her. She had called round to the house the night before, on her way home, to check the property. I was pretty frantic as you can imagine, and kicked up such a fuss that one of her colleagues ended up going round to her house to collect the keys. It got sorted in the end, but it added a lot of stress to the whole experience." Helen, 23

The previous occupants are still there

If this happens, it is likely that they are just running behind schedule and will soon be on their way. Staying cool and not losing your temper is the best way to chivvy them along. An offer of help may also be a sure way to get them moving – they won't want to be seen as deficient in the face of your obvious organisational skills. Psychologically speaking, we don't like to be seen as further down the social desirability ladder than others (i.e. we like to think that we are better than others at things that are valued by society), and we will attempt to redress any perceived imbalance – if this means getting a move on, then so be it.

Another tactic is standing outside the property and alternately staring at your watch and the house. This is a technique that any stalker may be familiar with, but not one we recommend. It is just as likely to make people more bloody-minded and 'go slow'.

People Watch: moving day helpers

Many hands make light work, so they say. However, unless they're managed well your moving day helper could become the proverbial millstone around your neck. Below are suggestions for managing different types of happy helpers.

The Macho Helper

Typically, this helper uses your house moving as an opportunity to show how strong, tough, virile and masculine he is. He will (and it is always a he) insist on shifting the heaviest boxes – alone – turning down any sensible offers of help. He sees suggestions about lightening his load as a challenge to his masculinity, and may even take that as a cue to double his burden just to prove how 'hard' he really is.

Psychologically speaking, this person is probably insecure about his masculinity and seeks any opportunity to assert his male superiority and tough guy image – especially if there is an adoring female audience present. The Macho Helper can be a liability and needs to be managed carefully. This can be done by admiring his flexed muscles, whilst at the same time steering him towards lighter boxes and offers of help, so that he doesn't injure himself and take up more of your precious moving time.

The Organiser: *"Come on! You're 17 seconds late loading that tea chest into the lorry."*

The Organiser

This person knows what has to be done, how it should be done, and has the lists to prove it. Now in moderation, lists are a good thing. But the Organiser will have a list for all possibilities and eventualities, and these lists may also appear on a computerised master list of lists. They will be forever checking things off lists, and preventing you doing things that are not in the correct order – even to the extent of disallowing unauthorised toilet breaks.

What you have here is a bona fide control freak. In psychological terms, this is a person who only feels comfortable when they are in control of a situation – they are highly intolerant of disorder. This can, of course, be used to your advantage, as they will probably do a fine job if you let them. However, their inflexibility could be bad for your bladder...

Manage the Organiser by making a show of acquiescing to their organisational superiority when it suits your purpose, but introduce an element of flexibility into proceedings even if means sneaking off to do your own thing when they're not looking.

The Commentator

The Commentator feels a need to provide a grating, running narrative on the whole proceedings – usually in a shrill and pedantic tone. They insist on describing everything as it happens, even to the extent of pointing out the blindingly obvious ('Oh look, that box has just burst open and look at you, you're all covered in flour').

Psychologically speaking, they probably have a deep seated need to get involved with a situation without getting their hands dirty and without having to go to the effort of thinking of anything useful or insightful to contribute.

Manage the Commentator by giving them an out-of-earshot job to do, such as assembling boxes in the garage or packing up the potting shed (or counting cat's eyes on a nearby motorway).

The Critic

There's always one. The Critic is always telling you how it should have been done rather than offering constructive input. They will tell you how you should have packed the boxes, that you should have confirmed arrangements in triplicate, and that the removal people you have chosen are nothing more than a bunch of cowboys.

Psychologically speaking, this person is insecure and needs to assert their superiority by putting others down. They are likely to have self-esteem issues, and need to boost their fragile egos by appearing to know best.

There are two ways to manage the Critic – the long way and the short way. The long way is to try to justify to them why you have done things the way you have, but be prepared for a long day. The short way is to call their bluff – ask them to do it for you instead – ask them to pack the damn box then. They will probably back down.

The Shirker

The Shirker tries very hard to look like they're helping, but always mysteriously appears after the hard work is done. They will take oodles of time over the easy tasks, and make a whole song and dance about it. When it comes to the tough tasks, they will claim to be preoccupied with, or exhausted from, prior activities. They have this down to an art form – it is a thing of beauty to behold – if you weren't so damn pushed for time. They are full of gusto for a task when it is already finished, and they will vent some (un)righteous indignation that you did it without them ('I was going to help, honest, why didn't you wait...?').

Psychologically speaking, this person is simply lazy, but still wants to get the credit. This person is a Social Loafer – they don't pull their weight if they don't have to or if they can possibly get away with it.

Manage the Shirker by giving them responsibility for, and psychological ownership of, a particular task. By doing this, they can't offload it on to somebody else.

Top Tips to surviving moving day

1 Try not to take your stress out on other people. Moving house is one of the most stressful life events that you will encounter, and knowing this is half the battle – so don't delude yourself into thinking that

the day will go well: the chances are it won't. Expect stress and it won't be able to creep up behind you and take you by surprise.

2 Make it fun – try to keep your sense of humour intact. Laughing about the removal man's 'builder's bottom' or overhanging beer gut can be a good bonding experience.

3 Remember to keep your mind focused on the greater goal of moving day. Soon you will be ensconced in your new home, and the troubles of this particular day will be a long distant memory.

4 Don't expect everything to fall into place straight away – a lot of people are intolerant of disorder and chaos, and like everything to have a place before they can relax. If you are such a person, be aware of the 'Expectation Gap'. This is a psychological phenomenon that accounts for the deficit between the ideal and current situation. The larger the gap, the more uncomfortable we feel. The only way to reduce the gap is to either change your expectation or change the situation. As changing the situation may well be beyond your control, you will probably need to lower your expectations.

5 Give yourself a treat/goal to work towards. For example, book a meal out that night at one of your new local eateries. Some people with Type A tendencies (see Chapter 8) might find it hard to leave a job (like unpacking) unfinished so if this is you, see such a diversion as necessary for exploring your new area i.e. as an important part of the moving process (don't forget that a bottle or two of wine with the meal is just as necessary).

Of course this is an idealised plan for dealing with moving day. If, however, you are the fortunate owners of small (or not-so-small) children then a whole different range of factors enters the equation...

CHAPTER 6

Moving with kids (and other animals)

Bickering. Petulance. Tantrums. Moodiness. Even aggression. No, we're not talking about the behaviour of your spouse during moving time but that of your kids. Whether you are moving down the street or two hundred miles away (or even to another continent), children suffer, even more than humans, from the lack of stability, familiarity and constancy in their lives. And if they suffer, you suffer. Read on to discover how applying a bit of psychology can go a long way to making the transition run more smoothly for all.

Before the move

The key to a successful move with kids is to keep them in the loop as much as possible. Many parents try to protect their children, especially younger ones, by not giving them too much notice about an impending move for fear that they will have too much time to 'worry' about what will happen. It is, in fact, far better to introduce the idea gradually, in stages, with plenty of time for them to absorb the information prior to the move. An airy 'By the way, we'll be sleeping in a different house/city/country tonight and you'll never see your friends again' as the removal men drive up, is not the way to go.

10/10 **Top Ten pre-move strategies**

1 Acknowledge that things will change. Denial or attempts to minimise change are not helpful. It is better to discuss the changes
that will happen and how they might affect different parts of their
lives such as friends, school, bedroom and so on.

2 Take the time to explain why the move is necessary. Don't try to
hide anything – kids have inbuilt radar systems to pick up on any
attempts at subterfuge. So if the move is for your work, don't pretend it's for the children's benefit. If they realise you are being less
than honest about your motivations for the move, they may suspect
your honesty elsewhere too.

3 Present a united front even if one of you has reservations about the
move; for example, if the move is to be nearer 'Daddy's work', they
may blame Daddy for all woes associated with the move. Make it
quite clear that Mummy thinks it's a good idea too.

4 Encourage them to talk and express their fears and worries. Don't
whatever you do dismiss them by telling them not to be 'silly' or
that everything will be 'OK'.

5 Involve them as much as possible in the process. Let them come
with you on property visits in the later stages if possible (but probably not if the children are very noisy, smelly and leaky). Let them
choose the décor for their new room (as long as they're not going
through a Goth phase). Take them to visit the new area and suss
out the school, the parks and so on.

6 Point out the positives in the move. More space, bigger bedroom,
own bedroom, better garden, better local facilities – whatever positives you can find, accentuate them.

7 Don't force them to throw away all their 'junk'. They may need to
cling to their memories in the face of an uncertain future. Their history is an important link with the past so let them hang onto those
mangy childhood mementos (resist the temptation to slip the
removal men a fiver to 'lose' them).

8 Help them create a memory book of their old house. They could take photos, draw pictures, interview neighbours etc. This helps them maintain their sense of identity and can offer comfort in unfamiliar territory. Best not let them rip strips of wallpaper off to stick in their book though.

9 Give each child an age-appropriate task to do before the move. This could be responsibility for packing up one room or sorting through a box of toys. It could be searching the Internet for information about your new neighbourhood; it could even be, for older children, sourcing a removal firm. Just don't give them the task of looking after the keys for the new property. For obvious reasons.

10 Give them a Moving House Present. This will obviously depend on your budget but should be something special for them. The gift should evoke positive emotions which should mean that they will associate those emotions with the house move. Hopefully.

Moving day

Moving day is stressful for everyone but all that waiting around with nowhere to hang their hat can affect kids' delicate psychological constitution more than most. Here are the most important pointers:

- Make sure that you allow them time to say goodbye – to their friends, neighbours and yes, even their room. You might feel a bit daft saying 'bye bye wall' with your toddler but they won't (best not do this with your teenager though).

- Make sure that they have access to (healthy) food which is a challenge when your fridge is disconnected, your cupboards bare and your chocolate Hobnob collection is crumbling away at the bottom of a large box labelled 'dry goods' (or possibly, for real Hobnob fans, labelled 'chocolate Hobnobs'). Go out for a meal or order a takeaway (don't have to worry about spills on the carpet for once – ha!).

- Let them keep treasured possessions to hand. This helps maintain a link between the past and the future and also lets them cling (literally, in the case of tatty old Teddy and other 'snugglies') to something familiar.

- Unpack the kids' things first so that they can feel settled quickly. This means that you need to have their boxes to hand which takes some advance planning.

After the move

Change is unsettling for many people, but even more so for kids. They may react in different ways. Like adults, some will take it all in their stride. Others may revert to childish behaviours (will you be able to tell the difference?) such as sucking their thumb, talking in a 'baby' voice or becoming clingy. Younger ones may revert to bed-wetting whilst older ones may suffer mood swings, aggression or anxiety. School performance may be affected and some kids may develop (real or imaginary) stomach aches or headaches.

Here are some tips to make things as easy as possible:

- Establish familiar routines as soon as possible. Children thrive on routine and knowing what will happen when, makes them feel safe.

- Organise a treat or something special as soon as you can post-move. Cinema, pizza, making chocolate cornflakes...whatever does it for your child. Maybe even get a pet to occupy them and give them something to care for (if you don't want poo all over your new carpet, make it a goldfish, or even better, buy a virtual pet like a Tamagotchi).

- Encourage their old friends to visit or arrange for them to go back and see their old haunts. This may not be terribly practical if you have moved to another country, of course – use email to keep in touch with people left behind instead. Also, be careful about going back to your old house; children may find it distressing to see a new family sloshing around as if they own the place (which, of course, they do). And you may find it distressing to see what they've done to your lovely petunias or garden path.

- Visit local attractions as soon as possible – even before you have unpacked everything. Check out sports facilities, enrol them in scouts or cubs, find out if there are any art or music classes etc.

- It might be a good idea to keep their old bed or a special piece of furniture such as a chest of drawers to maintain a sense of continuity between their old and new life.

Tips for moving with baby

Babies are probably the easiest to move. Their sense of security depends entirely on the close proximity of their 'primary care giver', who, for the sake of simplicity, we'll call Mum (but could equally be Dad and is most likely to be both). The other essential for babies is routine; as long as they have Mum close by and have a stable routine, you could probably take them to the moon and back without them being too bothered.

The problem is in maintaining a routine when all around you is descending into chaos. How do you put them down in their cot with the curtains closed if the cot (or curtains) are packed? If it is Daddy who normally bathes them but he is preoccupied with trying to manoeuvre a six foot bed down a narrow staircase, the normal routine goes out the window (and so might the bed, if things go really badly). So, clearly, sticking regimentally to Baby's routine is not totally practical. Some tips then:

- If Baby does have a very strict routine that will be impossible to maintain during the move, make sure you vary it in the days or weeks running up to moving day. Make sure that it isn't Dad who always bathes her, or Mum who always reads the bedtime story.

- Pack the baby's things last and take them with you (where possible) so that you can unpack them first.

- Consider farming Baby out to a familiar adult on moving day as change can be very unsettling. This obviously depends on the age of the child and how much they are used to being away from their primary care giver.

"Now, are you sure we haven't forgotten anything?"

- Keep Baby's favourite toys, soothers and snugglies close to hand. Also, their favourite cups, bottles, bowls and so on so that their routine stays as familiar as possible.

- Avoid other transitions at this time such as weaning, introducing cup to replace bottle, move from crib to cot, move from bouncy chair to high chair etc.

- Talk to your baby about what's happening – even if you don't think they understand. They will pick up on your emotions so explain over and over again in an upbeat voice about the new house, their new room etc.

Baby may well become more clingy following the move, especially with their primary care giver. They might reject Dad or other people, as they cling desperately to the main constant in their lives; this is normal and is simply a way of obtaining reassurance that Mum won't change and disappear on them like their old house did. A lot of mums wonder whether it would be a good idea to let their child sleep with them at this time, especially if they do seem extra clingy. There are two school of thoughts on this – basically, 'yes' and 'no'.

Some argue that bringing them into your bed starts a habit that is hard to break whilst, psychologically suggesting to the baby that there must be something to be fearful of if they are suddenly allowed to sleep with Mummy and Daddy. Others feel that offering your baby extra reassurance at this time is psychologically more healthy than leaving them alone in a strange place. Probably the best option is to settle them in their own room, but reassure them with your presence every time they need it (which is likely to involve a lot of interrupted sleep for you). Over the next couple of nights, gradually phase out the continual reassurance so that you might, for example, take longer to come into their room, stay a shorter time, make less eye contact and say less each time.

Helping toddlers and pre-schoolers cope

Pre-schoolers and toddlers are old enough to know what is happening but not old enough to really appreciate the full ramifications of the move or to understand why it is necessary. The good thing is that they aren't yet settled into schools, so disruption is minimised. Attachments to playmates might be strong, but kids of this age quickly make new friends and have great resilience when it comes to social contacts – introduce a potential playmate who has their own toy Teletubbie and they'll bond for life.

However, small children can feel deeply unsettled by an impending move. Their concept of time is rather vague, so telling them that they are moving in three weeks means little to them. Crossing off days on a calendar can help, as can counting how many 'sleeps' until moving day.

It is probably best not to give too much advance warning of the move with very young children who are liable to either forget all about it ('But I told you six months ago' won't help) or repeatedly ask three times a day if today is The Day (three months of that and you'll probably be driven to cancel the whole damned thing).

Saying goodbye for young children has to be handled well. It is important for them to have 'closure' to help them understand that their life will change irrevocably, but too many tears and too much distress from the 'left behind' is clearly disturbing. So, farewell parties at nursery or playgroup are fine and dandy, but make sure that the staff or carers talk enthusiastically about the new life they will lead, rather than lamenting about what they will miss in their old one. Similarly, saying goodbye to friends should be upbeat and cheerful, hopefully with less of an emphasis on 'finality' than at nursery. For example, you can reassure your child that they can speak on the phone to the 'left behind', or perhaps visit (don't lie though).

As with older children, always stress the exciting possibilities that the new life will offer, emphasising the new play areas, parks, playgroups etc. Where possible, take them to visit before the move, pointing out all that is wonderful (and hope they won't notice the less than wonderful – like their smaller room or the longer walk to the park).

As with babies, any time near moving day (including at least a month either side) is not the time to be embarking on new stages such as potty training or moving from a cot to a big bed. Similarly, keep to their normal routine as much as possible and, where it is not possible, try to make the changes seem like exciting adventures (eating picnics on the floor, having a shower rather than a bath etc). Here are some more tips:

- Ensure that young children have their favourite toys and comfort objects close by. Let them choose a small selection of toys to see them through the actual move (before the rest of their stuff is unpacked).

- Give them a job to do so they feel involved rather than just shooing them away all the time. Suitable jobs include filling packing boxes with anything, from pots and pans, to toys and clothes. Make sure you don't leave anything dangerous around such as kitchen knives or cleaning fluids. You can't expect any very expert packing so you may have to repack all their efforts when they don't notice – or else risk having one huge box with a rather forlorn Flopsy the Rabbit at the bottom of it and another box so jam packed with toys that it is impossible to close.

- Other good jobs include sticking labels (or even just random stickers) on boxes (but not writing them), colour coding stickers by colouring them in, and sorting through toys to see which, if any, can be got rid of.

- Read books together about moving house. This is a good time to encourage your child to express their worries or concerns.

- Make sure that they understand that belongings being boxed WILL (you hope) reappear in your new home; young children may think they will never see all their familiar stuff again.

- If you have been on holiday with your child, make sure that they understand that this move is different and that your 'hotel' will be your new every night home. Actually, when many kids are toddlers, they often think that holiday hotels are to be their new homes forever; they always seem amazed to be back home, as if they never expected to see their house again – a prospect that bothers them not a jot.

- Have them send themselves a postcard or letter (for older ones) to arrive at their new home. They will be inordinately excited at the prospect of getting to the new house to see if it has arrived.

- Children this age can worry about being left behind. This may seem an absurd worry (unless you have several kids in which case it might seem only too feasible) but you must treat this and any other improbable concerns seriously.

Helping primary aged kids with the move

Once children reach five, you introduce the extra dimensions of a new school and social life into the melting pot of upheaval and disruption. The older children get, the more central their friends become to their happiness and well being, so any move that impacts on their social life is going to hit primary aged children harder. However, don't despair – at this age kids are still very resilient and generally open to new experiences and friendships. Most local primary schools have a steady trickle of new inmates each year – most of whom settle in and make new friends surprisingly quickly.

Children this age are obviously more able to reflect and project than pre-school kids, so are able to consider the implications of the impending move more thoughtfully. They are aware that they will be missing an old, familiar life and may seem disproportionately upset about missing particular events, such as a forthcoming sports day or classmate's party; it might seem to you that such minor events are two-a-penny but it is what their absence will symbolise that is likely to so upset children. A party or school event without them means that life is brutally intending to carry on without them and that can be hard for fragile senses-of-self to absorb.

Changing schools can seem very daunting for primary age children (and for their parents) as they have to get used to new uniforms, new rules and regulations, different curriculums (perhaps), new methods of teaching and, of course, new friends. And you will have to take a more active role in helping your child through the early stages than you might with a teenager. Here are some tips to help your child through the transition:

- Try and visit the new school in advance. If possible, ask that a letter goes out to your child's new classmates to introduce the newcomer and perhaps giving a contact phone number or email address so that children can start making friends as soon as possible (see below).

"We moved to a new region with our seven year old daughter at the start of the summer school holidays. The Head Teacher sent a letter out to all the kids in Chloe's new class explaining that she would be joining them in September and adding our phone number in case anyone wanted to invite her to play over the holidays. Nothing happened at first but then she got invited to a birthday party. From that, a few other invites followed and by the time she actually started school in September, she had a few tentative friendships. Now, one year on, her best friend is that child who extended that first birthday invite." Jackie, 39

Moving with kids (and other animals)

- Be proactive in helping your child make friends. Get friendly with other mums in the playground (sorry to be sexist about this, but whilst dads certainly are a regular feature in most school playgrounds, we have yet to hear of many dads actually making social arrangements for their children; there is something about the Y chromosome that seems to preclude this) and make play dates or social plans for your kids. Of course, you should check with your child first before inviting strangers over that they are expected to play with.

- Encourage your child to join after-school clubs or attend activities at sports or youth centres. This will broaden their interests and give them far more opportunities for developing friendships. In a class of 25, your child may flounder amongst long standing cliques, but enrol her in an activity that only a few of her classmates attend and she will become part of their 'in-group' much quicker.

- Allow them to stay in touch with old friends and their old life. E-mail is brilliant for this, as is texting and plain old-fashioned writing. Encourage return visits if possible, although it would be better for the old friends to visit you rather than the other way round. Chances are your child's old buddy will be the best ally you have in persuading her that this new life is cool.

Teenagers – the most difficult age of all?

Yes, we suspect that they really are the most difficult to move. In fact, you might be better off leaving them behind with a good, strong cardboard box to curl up in under the railway arches. If your conscience won't allow that (oh, don't be such a softie), then follow our advice to help you move your reluctant and rebellious teenager.

First, let's see the world through their eyes. Your teen has an active social life – probably far more active than yours. They have a complex and busy school life – probably far more complex than your work life. If they have a girl/boyfriend, they may have an active sex life – yes, probably far more active than yours.

Bottom line – what's in the move for them? They are not interested in a bigger house or better local facilities, and, in characteristic teenage egocentricity, they definitely do not care about your need to relocate for work reasons. Most teenagers are affiliatory, pack animals who rely on their mates for everything from opinions and values to entertainment and gossip. They may have cultivated bonds with their peers over many years, and you want to come along and sever them by upping sticks and moving house. What are you thinking?

Well, if the above hasn't incited you to hastily withdraw your house offer and cancel the removal men, then follow these pointers to help minimise the pain (for you as much as for your teenager).

- If they are pining for a girlfriend or boyfriend, don't even try to offer words of comfort. Proclamations about fish in the sea (of which there are plenty more), or puppy love, will NOT be helpful. Best to just give them space whilst being encouraging (and, perhaps less than truthful) about the success rates of long distance romances.

- Talk to them about the reasons for moving. Don't expect them to throw their arms around you and say, 'I *so* understand, Mum,' but it still helps to go through it all.

- Don't minimise their distress. Parents, with the wisdom that only age can bring (or a few *very* bad experiences), know that people move on, that new friends will be made and that, especially, new young love will be found. None of that is relevant to your furious 14 year old who is adamant that she will never be happy again. She will, but don't dismiss her feelings too easily.

- Ensure they have the means to stay in touch with their old pals as much as possible. For example, make sure you get the computer online as soon as possible for emailing/Instant Messaging, make sure that the credit is topped up on their mobile (and perhaps a little more credit than usual is called for), and try to arrange return visits or exchange visits where possible.

- At the same time, you'll need to walk a fine line between allowing them to take comfort from the life they have left behind and encouraging them to move on and forge new friendships.

Leaving teens behind

Whilst the earlier reference to leaving your teenager behind in a cardboard box was a joke (honest), many families do decide to leave older teens behind in the care of a responsible adult – such as close relative or family friend. This may be the best alternative if moving is likely to cause major disruption to their education (e.g. just before A Levels) or if you don't feel that an unavoidable move at this stage is in their best interests. Managing this process can be tricky, with issues such as finances, access and parental responsibility needing to be considered. Generally, it is best to have someone act in loco parentis in your absence, but a 17 year old may rebel against this and want to rent their own place with mates. Obviously, your feelings on this will depend on their age and maturity, as well as who is around to keep an eye on them.

However independent older teens may want to be, they still benefit greatly from an 'anchor' that is the parental home. Just as University students always have the back-up of going back home for weekends or at term end, so your left-behind teen could well benefit from having a designated place in your new home to call their own.

Moving and separated families/step-families

Complications can arise when the move involves family break-ups or mergers with new families. Children may have to cope with leaving dad (or mum) and/or other siblings behind or with acquiring a new parent (and possibly accompanying children). Dealing with the emotional fallout connected with such situations is beyond the scope of this book; however, it is important to recognise the issues and difficulties that can arise. Where possible firm links should be made with those left behind and consideration taken of the distress involved. This may be especially difficult given that you are probably going through a traumatic time yourself.

Moving with pets

Moving house with pets such as cats and dogs can be traumatic for them. Rabbits, hamsters and budgies fare rather better – whilst goldfish rarely present many problems. So, unless you fancy trading in your beloved spaniel for a long haired guinea pig, you will need to plan the move as carefully as you would do with kids.

Assuming you are uprooting your pet and replanting him within the same country, then there are some simple ways to make things easier. The best option is probably to book Tiddles or Rover into a cattery/kennels during the actual process of the move so you don't have to worry about him escaping or curling up for a sleep in the box labelled 'For The Skip'.

However, this route might be deeply unsettling for some animals, especially if they have never boarded before. Even if they have, to emerge from their 'holiday' and find themselves taken to an entirely new home that smells and looks entirely different, is probably unnerving. Cats and dogs are a bit like small children however (except a little less demanding), and are usually happy as long as their loved ones are close by. So, like children, they may be a little more clingy in the days following a move as they learn to accept their new environment.

Show your pet round their new home, talking to them about what each room is for (this probably does very little for them, but has enormous psychological benefit for you). Keep them on a lead for the first few times that you take them out and show them their new neighbourhood. As with toddlers, a security blanket or toy that they have had since puppyhood/kittendom, is probably a good thing to tuck into their basket (which should not be new, however tatty and smelly it might have become).

Final tips: put your mobile phone number and new address on their collar or chip as soon as possible, and never give in to their pathetic whining at night by letting them into your bed. That goes for the toddler too.

So, you've moved your stuff, your kids are coping well (hopefully) with the idea of a new home and now it's time to go about the task of settling in...

CHAPTER 7

Settling in

'Every Englishman's Home is his Castle.' So the politically insensitive old saying goes, and for most of the population in Britain it's true. The majority of us demonstrate a pressing psychological requirement to feel secure and settled in our home: this need for shelter is a basic human need. And, of course, what could be more disruptive than moving everything you possess (and perhaps a little more besides – what do you mean you didn't return the lawnmower you borrowed from your old neighbours?) across vast distances and then be required to fit it all back in to a new abode that may well be woefully deficient in the nooks, crannies and cubby holes that you came to rely on in your old haunt?

Add to all this the need to ensure that we have our essential services on tap in our new home when we arrive – from electricity and gas, to milk and newspaper deliveries – and we have a dreadfully trying time thrust upon us. And that's even before we start to work out whether our neighbours are hostile and carnivorous, or friendly and herbivorous.

So what advice can psychology proffer the beleaguered travellers to settle them into their new home?

The psychological pressure to unpack – an itch that needs scratching?

The first thing that most people want to do once they have moved is to unpack all their stuff. This panders to our drive to feel settled and secure – as well, of course, as needing to know where our clean undies are. It is easy to be overwhelmed by the mountain of packing crates and boxes that cast their daunting shadows across the virgin canvas that is your new home. The best way to tackle this seemingly Herculean task is to break it down into more manageable chunks. One way is to do this by room, with the most psychologically important being the bedroom: we need to know that we have a place to lay our weary bones at the end of the tiring move day. Unpack the duvet and sheets, make the bed, hang the curtains and, hey presto, you now know that when you are so tired from unpacking the rest of the boxes (as you will be), you have somewhere to flop without any further exertion needed.

Some people are not happy until absolutely all of their boxes are empty and everything has a place. These people are driven by a need for order and control, and are very intolerant of chaos ('The Control Freak'). Some people are quite content to live out of crates for weeks, if not months: this type of person ('The Slob') is more easy going and tolerant of disruption. However, most of us tend to unpack the bulk of our belongings quite quickly and then spend about a year trying to ignore the final few boxes whose home in the new scheme of things never really becomes obvious (where *can* you put that mahogany boomerang which you so carefully carted back from Down Under?). A problem can arise when a Slob is moving with a Control Freak – then watch the fur fly. The best way to deal with this situation is to compromise – perhaps have one room designated as a dumping ground to appease The Slob whilst the rest is super tidy for The Control Freak.

Making your new house your home

There is a positive plethora of things you can do to make yourself feel truly comfortable in your new home.

1 Wipe away all traces – or at least the more obvious and perhaps more unpleasant ones – of the old occupants. The most effective way to do this is to clean every room yourself, dump any bits and pieces left behind, and then ultimately paint the rooms in colours that suit your tastes. Of course, if you've been clever in your choice of property, you will have selected a new home that has recently been painted in the colour scheme of your dreams (in which case you just need to clean).

2 Personalise your new home – this is the human equivalent of a dog cocking its leg and marking its territory. Place pictures and knick-knacks that make you feel comfortable throughout the house – so wherever you go, you see objects and artwork that says 'Yes, I'm here to stay'. Equally you should get rid of any items that the old occupants have left behind – unless you have a special reason for keeping them (such as a water feature in the garden that you particularly like, and without which you'll have to put your Koi carp in storage whilst you dig another pond).

3 Fill the house with sounds and smells that have a special meaning to you – though of course if you have kids or pets, this will be automatic (and not entirely welcome perhaps). Set up your music centre and play your favourite music as you unpack: soon the pleasant memories attached to the music will transfer to your new home. Cook your favourite meal so that the house is filled with tantalising and memory evoking odours, and so that when you sit replete after your first meal, your memories are good ones. The positive associations attached to your favourite pasta dish, or your beloved roast beef dinner, will soon establish themselves in your psyche as belonging to your new home.

4 Do something fun (e.g. throw a housewarming party, have a girlie/lads night in, or 'christen' each room with your partner...) in your new house as soon as possible, in order to plant the seeds of good times in your consciousness.

Setting up the essentials

If you enjoy waddling downstairs on a weekend morning to reap the bounty of the letterbox, i.e. the newspaper, then you need to have located your local newsagent. They have the absolute power to start your day on a high or a low. Similarly, if you are of a more traditional nature and prefer your milk delivered to your door, a rummage through the local phone directory should do the trick.

Having established the daily essentials, you should now turn your attention to your long term fixtures, that is to say, your neighbours – traditionally those that dwell on either side, but it can also include a number of the houses that surround you. Whatever their location, your life will be so much simpler and easier if you have good relations with all of your neighbours. Or failing good relations, a serene state of neutrality may be just as acceptable. Be prepared to smooth the potentially ruffled feathers of your neighbours who are uncertain about the strange people that have landed to roost in the nest next door.

> **Our survey said...**
>
> Over 50% of respondents in our survey made a concious attempt to introduce themselves to their new neighbours. Over 70% reported that their neighbours were a friendly bunch too and went out of their way to introduce themselves. Some neighbours brought welcome cards and flowers, others just stopped by for a friendly chat, although one or two went a little too far by enquiring about what colour they were going to paint the lounge, or even asking how much they paid for the house. One new neighbour even repeatedly asked one of our respondents why they didn't have kids.

People Watch: your new neighbours

People are strange – as The Doors once lamented. Or *there's nowt so queer as folk* as the people round our way say. You're never sure just who you'll be stuck with over the fence/ wall/hedge/gravel.

So, who are your new neighbours then? Generally, there are four broad categories of potentially tricky neighbours that you may need to watch out for (we don't need to tell you about the ideal neighbour – you'll know one when you see one). Recognising their type will allow you to deal with them more effectively.

The Gossip

We all know the type: nattering over the garden fence, happily disseminating the fruits of their latest gossip gathering expedition to anyone unfortunate enough to be in earshot. No piece of neighbourhood news is too small to be gleefully seized, eagerly analysed and indiscriminately distributed (with a few judicious embellishments to ensure a good tale).

The Gossip is often motivated by a need to increase their self-importance. The point of gossip and secrets is that the gossip monger has knowledge of something that others don't. This gives a delicious feeling of power that some people (who perhaps lack power in other areas of their life) find intoxicating. Being privy to information or to secrets makes us feel special and important – and by sharing the secrets, we are able to ensure that others know just how special and important we are.

Deal with the Gossip by feigning interest just enough to give the impression that you are not aloof (otherwise you can be sure you will be the one gossiped about next). Limit the conversation by being firm but not too dismissive. Try avoiding eye contact, don't ask any follow-up questions and be comfortable with silences. Of course, you don't want to cut them off completely because one day you might find out something useful (like the couple at the end of the terrace are planning a rock festival in their back garden next Bank Holiday Monday).

The Nosy Parker

The first sign that you are in the presence of the Nosy Parker is the twitching net curtain; you might not spot it the first time you leave your new home, or even the second time, but by the third time, you will feel that slight nagging sensation that you are being watched. Over time, your suspicions will be confirmed as you realise that your every move is being monitored, logged and probably subject to in-depth analysis. Your initial reaction may well be one of irritation as you lament the loss of your privacy. Fortunately, unlike the Gossip, the Nosy Parker doesn't feel the need to share the fruits of their labour with all and sundry.

The Nosy Parker may be motivated by the psychological need to feel in control of their environment. They want to know what is going on around them in case it impinges in any way on their ordered and secure daily life. Additionally, they may simply lack sufficient stimulation in their own lives and are looking to fill a void by using other people's comings and goings as a substitute for the paucity of their own.

However, do not underestimate the potential benefits of having the Nosy Parker next door (see below). They could well be the next best thing to having a burglar alarm. It is well worth fostering good relations with such a neighbour as long as you can cope with them knowing more about your life than your own mum does. The Nosy Parker can also be damned useful at taking deliveries in for you while you're at work (but be warned, they may well take a peek).

"We had bought a house in a crescent in which most of the neighbours were very friendly – it is hard to leave the house without stopping for a chat with any of the neighbours, which is nice but makes it necessary to add 5 minutes on to the journey time. As most are retired and spend time in the garden, they also make a very handy neighbourhood watch." Rachel, 38

The Nosy Parker: *"I just opened your post for you while you were away to make sure there was nothing urgent that needed dealing with."*

The Loner

Unlike the Gossip who you can't get away from, a meaningful interaction with the Loner neighbour is a rare event. They may well nod at you on their way out, or even grant you a cheery wave, but that is as far as it goes. For whatever reason (whether it be they are shy, incredibly busy, or just antisocial) they do not appear receptive to friendship.

The Loner may appear aloof, but this may simply be a mask hiding a plethora of insecurities: they may lack the confidence needed to build relationships, they may think they have little in common with you to talk about, or they may even think that you won't want to talk to them.

The way to deal with the Loner neighbour is to make regular friendly overtures, but don't push it. Repeated attempts to coerce the Loner neighbour into joining you for 'drinkies' are more likely to send them scurrying for cover than get them out into the open. Of course, an alternative way of looking at the Loner is to actually see them as the Ideal neighbour. Leave them alone and they'll leave you alone, which is pretty much what a lot of people want in a neighbour.

The ASBO Magnet

The antisocial exploits of this type of neighbour leave you fantasising about slapping an ASBO on their door. They park their car in inconvenient places (such as across your driveway), they have loud late night parties/barbecues (to which you are not invited), they have visitors coming and going noisily at all hours of the day and night, and their kids treat your garden as an extension of their own.

Psychologically speaking, the ASBO Magnets are trapped in the egocentric stage of childhood development. This means that they find it hard to see things from another's perspective; they think their way is best, and are unwilling to listen to anyone else's opinion – just like your average pre-schooler.

Dealing with the ASBO Magnet is a very tricky prospect. Do you simply ignore them and hope they will move on in the near future, do you try to fight fire with fire and have your own all-night raves, or do you try to reason with them (under the assumption that they are, deep down, rational human beings)? See the section later in this chapter for some strategies that you might employ.

So, what are the top five tips for getting on with your neighbours?

1 Be polite – make a point of greeting your neighbours whenever you see them, and generally being well mannered. A nod, a smile and a simple 'hello' should set you off on the route to good relations. Being seen as aloof will not improve your chances of being included on their Christmas card list.

2 Try and make a connection with your neighbours – look for anything that you might have in common (the psychological principle of 'birds of a feather flock together'). The connection can be as complex as coming from the same distant part of the kingdom, which is far removed from where you now dwell ('You come from Giggleswick too? I didn't think anybody else had ever heard of it!'), or as simple as having kids of the same age and lamenting as to what a nightmare of a developmental stage they are currently going through. Any level of connection which gets you talking generally sows the seeds of good relations – however take care to ensure that it is a connection that they are happy to germinate: it may be that enthusing about the fact you both drive a Ford will not have the desired effect if your new neighbour really doesn't know anything about cars, or perhaps harbours deep seated desires about upgrading to a BMW.

3 If you're planning to do anything to your property that might affect them, have the common courtesy to inform your neighbours first – but don't ask them for their blessing. For example, if you are having minor building work carried out on your house or garden, you probably have no intention of changing your plans if they object (and this will simply rile them). Instead, your courteous forewarning allows them to plan and have some semblance of control over their lives. Thus, if building work might create vast quantities of flying dust, alerting them in advance will ensure that they don't hang the washing on the line that day. Perceived control over their lives is something that human-beings, and hence, hopefully, your neighbours, value highly.

4 Do something which is of benefit to them, and which you haven't been asked to do. Don't panic! This doesn't mean that you should rush round and paint the front of their house. It can be a small gesture indeed – such as rescuing their wheelie bin from the middle of the road where the thoughtful refuse collectors have left it. Considerate little gestures such as these can cement neighbourly friendship.

5 Send them a Christmas card – assuming that this won't give offence (such as if they are practising Jehovah's Witnesses). Or if you're unsure of their religious leanings, play it safe with a 'Season's Greetings' card. It will simply show your neighbours that you are thinking of them. But be warned – make sure you get their names right, and even more importantly, the names of their kids. Failure to do so could require you to read the section on dealing with problem neighbours sooner than you would have liked.

But, of course, it would be naïve to think that everything will always be quite that simple. You can try all of the above techniques and still find that they have no effect, or worse still that relations with your neighbours deteriorate further. Then what do you do?

When things go wrong with the Joneses

It would be an optimist indeed who believed that life with one's neighbours will always be wine and roses – inevitably there will be times when you are required to sup the bitter taste of vinegar and bear the sight of ugly weeds with respect to those that dwell next door. It may be that you get off on the wrong foot with your neighbours, or that relations worsen after one specific incident, or simply deteriorate over time. If this is the case, it may not be necessary to barricade yourself into your castle and expect war. If there is one topic that psychologists have investigated in detail, it is why people get into conflicts with one another, and how it might be possible to resolve such conflicts. We will not dwell too much on the former – let's assume the worst case scenario, that the damage has been done and that the cannons are loaded – but will instead turn our attention to how we might cause peace to break out.

One of the major causes of conflict is prejudice. As has been seen throughout history, prejudice can be due to many things including colour of skin, ethnicity or religion. Similarly, it is possible that conflict between neighbours is also due in no small part to some form of prejudice, whether it be due to the car they drive (e.g. a tatty old banger, or a smart Roller), the adornments in the garden (don't we all love garden gnomes?), or simply the 'type' of people they are perceived to be. Humans are very quick to jump to conclusions based on a very small amount of evidence, but very slow to change them: and any such change normally requires vast amounts of evidence even to begin to modify attitudes.

Psychologists have found that an effective way to overcome such prejudice is to develop a way to show that the conflicting parties are in fact more alike than they are dissimilar. Such positive action can usually succeed in dispelling misperceptions and ending conflict. So, if you're in dispute with your neighbours, and you genuinely want to end the conflict (if you don't there's nothing that psychologists can do for you – good luck in your fight), or at the very least return to a quiet life, then you need to find a way to highlight your similarity.

This can be done in a passive way: for example, if you happen to see your hellish neighbours attending the same events as you (e.g. the same neighbourhood watch meeting, the same school parent evening, the same social clubs, the same church), instead of ignoring or blanking them as your natural inclination might be, a simple acknowledgement (such as a nod of the head) may well get them thinking that you're not all bad if you have these same interests as them. Hopefully, once this seed has been sown a couple of times, it should start to become obvious that you are not so different from them. It will then be a small step to start a brief conversation with them at such a gathering – at the very least you should be able to talk about the event you're attending – and take it from there.

There are a number of other ways that you can attempt to turn the neighbours from hell into your new best friends. These include:

1 If you have a specific bone of contention between you and your neighbours that has led to the deterioration of your relationship, a way to mend the fence, as it were, is to bring in a neutral impartial mediator – in all likelihood, another neighbour with whom you both have a reasonable relationship. Although the mediator will have no power, they can help in a number of important ways: firstly, they may be able to reduce the 'emotional heat' associated with the deadlock; secondly, they can help to address misperceptions and re-establish trust. A good mediator could also propose novel compromises that put you both in a win-win position. An important point to mention here is that the mediator needs to be acceptable to both you and your neighbour.

2 Psychological studies have shown that relationships between warring factions can be improved by encouraging them to co-operate in order to achieve tasks that are unachievable by either party on their own. These are referred to as 'superordinate goals'. One particularly effective superordinate goal is resistance against a shared threat. This is the basis for alliances between nations, so should probably work between you and your neighbour. For example, if a local authority is proposing an undesirable recycling scheme, it would be an opportunity for you and your neighbour to unite against the common enemy. When the common threat has been vanquished, it is likely that you will have established a good relationship, or at least, will feel neutrality to one another rather than hostility.

3 On some occasions, bargaining may be the answer. Assuming that you both do things that annoy the other, you could each agree to cut down the irritating activities as a form of truce. For example, if your neighbour insists on having loud, late night parties at weekends, and you, in turn, have children who continually kick a ball against their wall, you could agree to meet in the middle and only allow your children to do this when the neighbours are not at home, if they will agree to cut the parties down to once a fortnight. You get the idea.

4 On other occasions, negotiation may be the order of the day. So, for example, if your neighbour insists on having regular bonfires preventing you from putting your washing out, rather than storming in and demanding that he stops this antisocial activity, simply ask that he gives you advance notice so that you can plan your drying schedule accordingly.

5 Being nice can also be an effective strategy to disarm a hostile neighbour. The Norm of Reciprocity dictates that it is of immense psychological discomfort to have someone be nice to you without being nice in return. This does not mean that you have to go over the top in your efforts to be nice, but it could be something as small as a cheery hello with a smile when you see them, or as generous as a small present at Christmas. Having been the recipient of your niceness, your neighbour should feel compelled to redress the balance in some way.

The Honeymoon Ends

It can sometimes be very difficult to adapt to life in your new abode – especially if you had lived in your previous residence for many years, or if you were reluctant to move in the first place (but were forced to by life circumstances or an incessantly wheedling and whining partner). It was probably the case for the first week, or maybe even a month, that the adrenaline rush of the novel circumstances was enough to keep you buoyant and your misgivings at bay. But at some point, the honeymoon will end, and you may begin to regret the move.

Our survey said...

Just over a third of respondents in our research admitted that there was a point after their move when they had doubts about whether or not they had done the right thing. Reasons given included spotting other more desirable properties, being unable to fit all their stuff in their new home, missing features of the old home (like driveways, garages, proximity to parks etc.) or problems with neighbours.

Having doubts about such a life changing event is normal. In fact, if you don't experience any qualms three to six months after moving you will probably be in the minority. The human brain deals with regrets by fooling ourselves out of the 'cognitive dissonance' that regrets bring. Cognitive dissonance is a term that psychologists use to describe the uncomfortable feeling of having two thoughts or ideas that are incompatible. For example, knowing that you have gone through all the cost and upheaval of moving house whilst at the same time realising this was a mistake are two psychologically incompatible notions. The discomfort that we feel can be reduced by changing one of these notions: you can't change the fact that you have moved so you are likely to convince yourself that the move was a great idea. So expect doubts as being par for the course, and rest assured that they will almost certainly pass.

10/10 Top Ten Tips on how to know when you have settled into your new home

1 You no longer get up in the middle of the night and find yourself halfway down the hallway before realising that you now have an en suite loo and thus you no longer need to make a semi-comatose midnight dash to the family bathroom. We all have mental representations of our surroundings in our head – psychologists call them mental maps – whether it be our route to work or the layout of our home. Changes to environment and routine require modification to our maps, and this can take time depending on circumstances. So don't despair that, several weeks after moving house, you still find yourself turning left out of your driveway to work when you should be turning right, or stopping at your old house rather than continuing on to your new one – you'll adjust in the end.

2 You can remember your new telephone number. There's nothing more embarrassing than having to look up your own number from a pocket diary, personal organiser, scrappy piece of paper in your inside jacket pocket, or the felt-tip scrawl on the back of your hand. It can be difficult to remember new numbers (telephone or house), but using mnemonics can be a good way to cope. Mnemonics are simply aids to help improve your memory – pairing images or meanings which have personal relevance to things you are trying to memorise. So, when it comes to trying to memorise your new telephone number, first try breaking it down into three chunks of two numbers instead of trying to remember six single digit numbers, and then assign a meaning to each pair of numbers. So if your telephone number is 169751: 16 – your daughter's age; 97 – the year in which you got married; 51 – the score (5-1) by which England beat Germany in that glorious World Cup qualifier that we'll never forget. And if you can build the three images into a picture, say of your daughter outside a church slotting one sweetly past the German goalkeeper, even better for your memory processes. Of course, if you can't remember how old your daughter is, you're truly screwed. So make sure that your mnemonics are really something personal and memorable to you.

3   Your post is now arriving on a regular basis rather than being subjected to the vagaries of the Royal Mail's redirection service.

4   You have some sense of history being made in the house – for example if your memory of the last time you had a takeaway was actually in your new home, then you will have begun to establish a feeling of permanence.

5   Speaking of takeaways... you know you're truly established in your new home when you know the location of at least five takeaway restaurants (and probably their phone numbers off by heart too), and can provide directions to the 'biggies', such as the Golden Archways and the home of the Colonel. Likewise, when you know the location of all the drinking establishments in your area – by far the most common landmarks that people use to give directions by – even if you don't drink in them, you know you're settled.

6   When you have got your pictures on your wall – whether it be family photographs, your favourite landscape, or even just some postcard art. This is especially true if they are pictures that have been brought from your previous home. This helps to transfer the good memories to your new house and makes settling in much quicker and easier.

7   When your toddler first sleeps through the night in their new room.

8   When work colleagues, friends and family stop asking you whether you've settled in to your new home.

9 When your house starts to get untidy and the clutter creeps in. You've gone beyond the stage of everything being neatly tucked away into its new home, and before you know it your house is over-taken by piles of papers, mounds of magazines and crates of clutter.

10 When you're thinking about whether it's time to move house again.

We knew we were settled in our new home when:

- *"I put a shoe rack next to the door and my dad made a comment about this being the first piece of furniture in its right place, which cut through the hectic day and made me realise that this was to be my home."* Lizzie, 31

- *"All our belongings were in the rooms we wanted them in, and once the curtains were up."* Amanda, 23

- *"I'd hung up the family photographs."* Rachel, 46

- *"I had a housewarming party for friends."* Felix, 44

- *"I mowed the lawn."* Trevor, 31

Hopefully, you have now settled comfortably into your new home, but some people do encounter more serious problems. The following chapter looks at some of the more common difficulties.

CHAPTER 8

Problems, problems, problems...

No matter how much of an optimist you are, you need to steel yourself to the cold reality that you will face problems with your move. Of course, if you are a pessimist, you already knew this. However, by recognising where the potential disaster zones of this major life event lie, it is possible to plan and reduce their impact.

Our survey said...

Our research uncovered a plethora of problems that house movers have to cope with. 20% had some kind of money transfer delay problem. 12% had problems with the removal firm, 13% found that previous owners were still occupying the property when they were wanting to move in and 18% found that the new property was not in the state they expected it to be (e.g. it was filthy, belongings had been left behind, fixtures removed etc.). Rarer setbacks include the chain collapsing, some form of damage to, or loss of, belongings.

Mortgage problems

Before you can think about moving, you need to have the finance in place. This is the time at which to build a good solid foundation for your moving experience. Be realistic about what you can afford. Some people recommend that you should stretch yourself to your limit to buy the best possible home that you can at the time you are looking to move. This is not always good advice.

Psychologically speaking, we all have a comfort zone for the many different aspects of our life – borrowing money is just one of them. It is important to recognise how you feel about borrowing large quantities of money. The chances are that if you are a person who is comfortable running up credit card bills, then you won't have any problem with stretching yourself to the extremes with the size of your mortgage. However, if you generally consider yourself to be more conservative when it comes to money matters (and you pay off your credit card bills completely each month – or don't even own a card), then you should not over borrow on the size of your mortgage. For peace of mind, you need to stick to a level of debt with which you are comfortable. Recognising the type of person you are will help diminish the mortgage problems you may later encounter.

The other aspect to bear in mind when arranging finance is that you need to consider how your life may change in the future. Whilst most of us don't possess crystal balls (or if you do, seek medical advice at once), we should still have an idea of where our future is heading. Ask yourself the following questions:

- Are you likely to get promoted in the near future and thus earn more?

- Is there a chance that you (or your partner) will need to take an extended absence from work (e.g. due to maternity leave or a career break)?

- Is your job secure and if not, could you weather the storm on savings or partner's income?

Negative answers to these questions mean you should be very wary of overextending yourself financially.

Disputes with agents, gazumping and other underhand ploys

So, you've found your house and put in an offer. It's the house of your dreams and you are happy to pay the asking price. However, don't let yourself yet believe that your prize is won. There are some very unscrupulous people out there – 14% of our respondents suffered from underhand ploys.

Gazumping, the dread word of house buyers of the 1980s, may have faded from the memory of many people, but it is a practice that is still very much alive and kicking. Gazumping occurs when you have put an offer in with the seller, they accept your offer, but at a later date, before the contracts are signed, they accept a higher offer from another buyer. At the time of writing, this practice, which some might consider morally reprehensible, is currently legal in England, Wales and Northern Ireland (but not in Scotland where the sale is considered legally binding after an offer has been accepted).

Estate Agents will claim that it is their professional duty to pass on any further offers to the buyers even after the seller has accepted your offer. However, there may be a number of psychological moves you can make to lessen your chances of being gazumped.

Firstly, ask the estate agent whether they have any further buyers currently interested in the property, and if so, can you please have their assurance that they will now be told that the property has been sold. Similarly, the estate agent should be asked to give an assurance that the property will immediately be taken 'out of their window' and no longer advertised for sale. If the estate agent either refuses to do this (by offering some fancy sounding excuse) or claims that they have already arranged a viewing with another potential buyer, you can begin to see that you may be on shaky grounds. If this occurs, you need to press the agent for specific details, such as 'How many other clients do they currently have interested?', 'When are the viewings?', 'When will they be taking the property off the market?'.

The more details you seek from them, the harder it will be for them to lie to you at a later date. Whilst it is not necessarily recommended that you record your conversations with a hidden mike (let's not get carried away here), it would be a psychologically sound move for you to be seen by the agent to be writing down their answers to your questions. You are then making your intentions quite clear to them: if they lie to you, they will be caught out. And by all means, feel free to repeat their answers aloud as you are writing them down ('So you will be taking the house out of the window as soon as you get back to the office') so there can be no room for doubt or misunderstanding in your mind, the mind of the estate agent, and if they are present (and you should try to ensure they are), the mind of the sellers.

Secondly, if you can, make sure the seller is present when you make an offer or accept the asking price. Try to conduct the business face-to-face. You might find this difficult to do as estate agents will try to keep you apart as much as possible. Again they will say that they are merely protecting their client but, at the end of the day, you are entering into an agreement with the seller and not with the estate agent.

A common psychological practice that sellers, egged on by their agents, employ is the 'Bait and Switch' technique of persuasion. Put simply, they hook you into agreeing to buy your dream house at a given price, and then once they realise that you really like the house, they put up their asking price, knowing that you have fallen in love with the house and will probably agree to pay a couple of thousand pound more.

"We put an offer in for our dream home and it was accepted. We were so excited that when we went to a party that evening, we couldn't

help telling our friends the good news. We even told them where the property was, which we realised immediately was probably not wise. A friend of a friend was there and she was very interested – it turned out that she was looking for a property on behalf of an out-of-town family member. She told us that she had recommended our house to these people but they hadn't acted. We were a little worried but after a few drinks, soon forgot it. A few days later, this friend rang us and told us that she was in a dilemma. It seemed that the estate agent had contacted her family and told them that an offer had been put in on our house and that they should put in a higher offer quickly. We were horrified, rang our agent and demanded that they immediately put in writing our accepted offer. We couldn't believe their underhand ploy which we would never have known about had it not been for a drunken conversation at a party."
John, 39 and Rachel, 36

Common estate agent scams

Estate agents do not get a very good press on the whole. Is this justified? See below.

Our survey said...

Over half of the respondents in our survey were unhappy with the performance of their estate agent. 22% claimed that their agent was a 'waste of space' whilst 32% felt that their agent could have done more to help them. Only 16% of our respondents claimed that their agent was 'helpful' with a further 29% rating the agent as 'quite helpful'.

12% of our survey respondents reported having problems with regard to estate agent disputes.

Here are some ploys that are used by the less reputable estate agents out there.

● Putting forward false offers to vendors: e.g. telling the seller about a fake low offer (which will be rejected) so as to prepare them psychologically for a slightly higher (but genuine) offer that would probably have been rejected outright without the comparison (see below).

"The Agent made up a lot of different potential buyers to rush us into buying a property because he knew we were first-time buyers."
Chloe, 23

"Did I say £230,000? Sorry, obviously I meant £320,000."

- Misleading surveyors: By telling surveyors that other properties in the area have sold for higher prices than they have, they encourage buyers to pay more than they should.

- Undervaluing houses: Elderly people living alone may be targeted by this scam which enables the agent (or most likely, their friends or associates) to buy up properties cheaply themselves.

- Overvaluing properties: This hooks sellers into signing up with the agent who later encourages them to accept a more realistic price that, perhaps, a more scrupulous agent would have valued it at in the first place.

- Lying about instructions from the vendor: see below.

"The estate agent rang six weeks after I had put the offer in to tell me that the house was being put back on the market as I had not moved quickly enough. I explained that it can take a while for solicitors to get things done, as he should know being in the business, and that I would be ready to move in about another week. But he refused to budge, telling me that it was the seller who wanted to put it back on the market. I had the seller's phone number and rang him. He said he had not instructed the agent to carry out any such action. It was the estate agent wanting his fee quickly." Stephanie, 34

Be aware that these tricks happen and be alert for any suspicious activity on the part of the agent. Our natural psychological instinct is to accept what people are telling us as the truth unless we have a very good reason to believe otherwise. This is called the 'truth bias'. We are bombarded with so much information on a daily basis that it is impossible to verify all of it. We take mental short cuts and label everything as being truthful unless we are given cause to doubt. You could overcome this natural tendency by adopting the opposite 'lie bias' whereby you assume that everything the estate agent tells you is false in some way unless you can verify otherwise. This is more cognitive work for you, but it may protect you in the long run.

Code of conduct for estate agents

Your estate agent should abide by the code of conduct of the National Association of Estate Agents (assuming they are a member – see Chapter 2). You can get a copy of this code of conduct by ringing the Association on: 01926 496800.

Solicitor problems

Nearly a quarter of the people we surveyed reported having problems with their solicitor.

"Our solicitor was absolutely useless. We had to do all the hard work ourselves, for example we had to phone the solicitor to tell her to phone the vendor's solicitor and we also had to tell her what questions to ask. Our solicitor seemed unable to think for herself. She had no initiative and no understanding of how important and stressful moving house was for us." Richard, 36

Here are some tips to reduce the likelihood of your solicitor causing difficulties:

- Bear in mind that because solicitors like everything in writing (to cover themselves legally), everything will take a lot longer than you expect. Give yourself plenty of time when expecting action from your solicitor.

- Where possible, only instruct a solicitor who comes personally recommended, whether it be from a friend, relative or colleague.

- Always speak to a named person when you have contact with their office. Make a record of all contacts you have made including dates, time of call and who you spoke to.

Sometimes you will need to chase up your solicitor as they don't seem to share your urgency. Do this in a polite but firm manner and bear in mind that because they deal with these matters on a daily basis they don't see them as the major life events that you do. If you can figure out a way to make a personal connection with your solicitor then this will likely expedite your dealings with them. For example, mentioning that they come highly recommended will probably flatter them and they won't want to shatter such an illusion. Probably.

Acts of God and other catastrophes

Some things are simply beyond your control and will happen no matter what precautions you take. All you can do for situations such as these is to have measures in place to facilitate the 'mopping up' operation.

For example, when you move don't cut costs. Make sure there's an overlap on your insurance between your new and old house, and that your belongings are insured for the transit between your old and new homes, even more so as the distance increases (see below). You might be forgiven for saving money on insuring your goods if you are moving just down the road or around the corner, but if you are moving half the length of the country where major motorways will come into play, you need to make sure you are insured.

"The night before we moved, the bathwater overflowed and went through the ceiling into the kitchen where all the boxes were packed. We had to take everything out, dry the boxes outside, and repack until the early hours of the morning. Thankfully, the home was still insured and the company came round and dealt with it." Tony, 34

Make sure that you don't fall foul of the 'it only happens to other people' principle. If the worst comes to the worst and it does happen to you, see our stress busting tips at the end of the chapter.

Top moving problems

According to Jeffrey Normie, the following are common problems that occur during the moving process:

1 Deeds not reaching the solicitor.

2 Solicitors not communicating with each other (they don't like speaking on the phone – they like to do everything in writing which slows things down).

3 Money transfer delay.

4 Owners causing problems by doing silly things like giving the buyers the keys before completion, or negotiating agreements on critical points without informing the estate agent.

5 When exchange and completion are on the same day this can cause problems with people being in transit with all their worldly goods and not being able to get in to their property.

6 And finally, it does happen that the owners are still in the property.

It happened to me

We are including a few real life stories of things that have gone wrong to other house movers in order to a) forewarn you and forearm you and b) to reassure you that if it all goes pear shaped, you are not alone.

"We moved into a brand new conversion from an old property. When we moved (in November) there was no heating and the roof was leaking. It was so cold and uncomfortable that we had to go to a hotel for the first night which was a disappointment to say the least." Nicola, 55

"We had a verbal agreement with the vendor (through their estate agent) that they would build a rear wall up before they left. When we

got the keys, we saw they hadn't done it. The estate agent wouldn't support our claim and denied all knowledge of the agreement. Always get everything in writing." Jessica, 31

"Our buyer paid the asking price and we agreed not to accept any further offers. As time went by, he wanted us to move out into rented accommodated or the deal would be off. Each week he screamed at the estate agents and threatened to pull out if we didn't leave – the completion date had already been agreed in advance and wasn't delayed at all. It all went through as planned in 11 weeks but he demanded £1,000 compensation for the fact that we hadn't got out sooner. We packed up ready to exchange and to hand over keys only to find that his solicitor hadn't finished the conveyancing so he wasn't ready to buy. He managed to blame us for this. He was so aggressive that no one at the estate agent's would deal with him and we had to deal with him direct. We ended up knocking £500 off to get rid of him." Andy, 34

"We were in a chain for six months due to a delay on the part of our buyer. When we were finally able to complete, we discovered that the seller of our new property had increased the price by £1, 000 and had another buyer interested. Our estate agent had failed to let us know this information." Belinda, 36

10/10 **Top Ten Tips for surviving the stress struggle**

1 Going into a situation with your eyes open always helps. Recognise before you start that moving house may well be a process full of troubles and strife. If you anticipate problems they are less likely to catch you unawares. A dose of optimism can be healthy but too much optimism can lead you into a state of psychological dissonance; this is the gap between expectations and reality. If that gap is too wide, an uncomfortable state of dissonance is created. Ensure that the gap is as narrow as possible by expecting some strife.

2 Identify your Locus of Control. If you are 'internal' you tend to blame yourself for all that goes wrong in your world. More 'external' people blame outside events or other people for any problems they encounter. For example, if you are gazumped, Internals would blame themselves for not getting it in writing/putting in a high enough offer etc; the External, on the other hand, would simply blame immoral vendors/fate etc. If you tend to have an internal Locus of Control, try to be a little more external and remember that some things are beyond your control.

3   Reduce your Type A tendencies. People with Type A personality tend to suffer from 'hurry sickness' in that they are impatient, always in a rush and want things to happen now. They find situations like delays, slow moving events and hold-ups very stressful. Their Type B counterparts are more likely to take unexpected problems in their stride. Become less Type A by forcing yourself to slow down generally (including slowing down your talking, eating, walking etc.) and by using cognitive reframing techniques (see next point).

4   Use Cognitive Reframing techniques to change the way you perceive events and setbacks, for example putting things into perspective e.g. by asking yourself how much the delay will affect you in five years time. Reframe 'wasted time' so that you see it as a useful window for planning, thinking, philosophising etc.

5   Do something that is incompatible with the stress reaction. Stress is an arousal mechanism so if you are experiencing a competing emotion, the stress is likely to be replaced. For example, if things are getting to you, do something to make you happy or relaxed. Find your metaphorical comfort blanket, whatever it might be (e.g. gorging on an entire packet of Jaffa cakes, quaffing the contents of a bottle of Baileys or losing yourself in your favourite trashy magazine/novel).

6   Distraction techniques should not be undervalued. Distraction is a valid psychological technique for reducing stress albeit, perhaps, temporarily. It interrupts the stress cycle by stopping you thinking about the stressor and thus preventing the continuation of the stress response. Good distraction activities will vary from person to

person but could include a round on the golf course (assuming you haven't packed your clubs), watching your fave film or having a good gossip with your best mate.

7 Exercise is a well documented stress reducer. The aim of the stress response is to produce extra energy to enable the body to engage in 'fight or flight'. This is the response that enabled our cave dwelling ancestors to run away from predators or, if they were feeling brave (and hungry), to stay and fight. This extra energy is less useful in the modern world, unless you intend running away from a nasty vendor or attacking your conniving estate agent with a rolled up wedge of house particulars (not something we'd recommend). Having all this pent-up energy with no release can be harmful as the extra hormones and glucose swilling around your veins can adversely affect your cardiovascular system as well as your immune system. Exercise is an effective way of using up this extra energy.

8 Progressive Muscle Relaxation is a proven means of reducing blood pressure which rises when we are stressed (in order to pump blood faster around the body). The idea with this is to progressively tense and relax each muscle in your body to ensure that you are physically relaxed. This will prevent the aches and pains, such as neck ache and headaches, which typically arise when we're stressed. Starting with your toes and feet and, working upwards, ending with your shoulders and neck, squeeze and tense each muscle in turn for about 10 seconds. Notice the feeling of tension in your body and be aware of how comfortable it feels when you relax each body part.

9 Declutter your mind by writing down all the things that are worrying you or that you are thinking about. For many people, stress comes from brain overload; worrying incessantly about things or obsessing about the same thoughts that are whirling in a destructive vortex around your mind. Go one step further by putting them into two columns; one that you can do something about and the other that you can't. For those that you can work with, devise an action plan. For those that you can't control, either allow yourself a limited amount of 'worry time' or write down a reason why you shouldn't worry about it.

10 Mobilise social support mechanisms. This includes having people (friends or family) to talk to, to offer practical and emotional support. Psychologically speaking there is merit to the old saying 'a problem shared is a problem halved' as research suggests that a support network can help you to cope with your stressful load. No matter how busy your moving schedule is, take time out to reconnect with friends and visit family. At the very least, texting can offer a surprising degree of emotional support.

Worldly Wisdom from house movers in our survey

We asked participants in our survey to pass on their pearls of wisdom about the moving process. Here are the more printable ones...

"Be philosophical about the whole process – if it's meant to be, it's meant to be."

"Expect delays and push your solicitors otherwise the process could be delayed further."

"Get a full survey done."

"Use a professional company to pack and move you."

"Ask around for someone who has been satisfied with their solicitor."

"Prepare for the worst, expect nothing to flow freely, never believe a word the vendor says, get everything in writing, and pay extra for the more expensive survey."

"Make yourself aware of the total cost of the move before you consider it as there are hidden costs that you don't even realise."

"Stay calm and get a good solicitor."

"Realise that everything takes longer than you think."

"Be very clear about what you expect of your partner and stick to it."

"When looking for a house, just drive around areas you like and note what houses are for sale."

"When buying a new property, get the building company to do your snags for you – it's well worth it."

"Lager – it really does help."

"Don't be too precious about the house you are leaving. The new owners will want to change it."

"Stay calm, wine comes in useful."

"Be organised, but don't pack too early."

"Remember that you're in it together and not to take the stresses out on each other."

"Find out where everyone else in the chain is going before you're awkward with them."

"Negotiate directly with the people buying/selling rather than going through an estate agent/solicitor – and keep on friendly terms."

"Always be prepared for the worst and then it can only get better."

"Take a day off, sit with lots of tea and ring up the gas, electricity and telephone with new details and meter readings. It takes so long to do...as so many companies take forever to answer the phone."

"Have a folder with old house details in it and a folder with the new house details in it. There is so much paperwork involved – if you leave it piling up in drawers, you're asking for trouble."

"Label your boxes, throw away as many of your possessions as possible before you move and practice your shouty voice for your solicitor."

"Pack one room at a time and mark all the boxes. Get your friends and family to help. Unpack straight away."

"Take an objective third-party with you on viewings."

"Contact you solicitor and estate agent on a daily basis – don't rely on them contacting you. Have a named contact."

"Tidy out your rubbish. Make it a positive occasion to clear out your life."

"Imagine living there at all times of the year."

"Remember that things can change with any surrounding land that doesn't belong to you."

"Moving house is a very stressful time so try and ensure that nothing else is happening around that time e.g. impending births."

"Dress the house you're selling; undress the house you're buying."

There, it wasn't so bad after all, was it? OK, it was, but don't say we didn't warn you.

Contact us

You're welcome to contact White Ladder Press if you have any questions or comments for either us or the authors. Please use whichever of the following routes suits you.

Phone: 01803 813343 between 9am and 5.30pm

Email: enquiries@whiteladderpress.com

Fax: 01803 813928

Address: White Ladder Press, Great Ambrook, Near Ipplepen, Devon TQ12 5UL

Website: www.whiteladderpress.com

What can our website do for you?

If you want more information about any of our books, you'll find it at **www.whiteladderpress.com**. In particular you'll find extracts from each of our books, and reviews of those that are already published. We also run special offers on future titles if you order online before publication. And you can request a copy of our free catalogue.

Many of our books have links pages, useful addresses and so on relevant to the subject of the book. You'll also find out a bit more about us and, if you're a writer yourself, you'll find our submission guidelines for authors. So please check us out and let us know if you have any comments, questions or suggestions.

Fancy another good read?

If you've enjoyed **Upping Sticks** how about finding out about moving to the countryside? If you're thinking of quitting the city life for a rural existence, check out Richard Craze's **Out of Your Townie Mind** *The reality behind the dream of country living.* The book takes the top 24 dreams of living in the country, based on a survey of city dwellers and ex-townies, and examines the pitfalls you need to avoid. From dreams such as having space and wide views or going for long walks, through to keeping chickens or having a big kitchen with an aga, Craze tells you how to make sure your dreams don't become nightmares.

Here's a taster of what you'll find in **Out of Your Townie Mind** If you like the look of it and want to order a copy, you can call us on 01803 813343, or order online at **www.whiteladderpress.com**.

Being near water

The Dream

Imagine. It is dawn. The lesser-feathered hoot calls forlornly across the marshes. The tide is out and the mudflats are alive with waders and dippers, catchers and plungers. Just out there, where the little waves lap, a small boat is moored, waiting. It is your boat. All you have to do is slip the oars, cast off and you'll be away, out into the bay, out into freedom. There is a little light mist rising and not a soul around to spoil this perfect dawn on the river; this perfect day by the sea. Overhead a heron glides majestically as it comes in to land light as a feather on the edge of the water where it feeds greedily. You hoist your one red sail and slip silently out into the main channel. You pull the collar of your midshipman's jacket up higher as the morning air is still cold but you feel alive, happy, content, smug. This is the life, messing about in boats, fishing, or just sitting and gazing.

The Reality

The dream can sometimes live up to the reality but often it doesn't because the reality has something missing, or has an extra something that we didn't take into account. I once took a young son of mine on a ramble along the sea shore and he seemed miserable and fed up. We did catch sight of a cormorant but that wasn't enough. He finally admitted he was disappointed as there was no music. And it was too windy. He was too used to watching nature programmes on the telly where you did get music and it was never windy.

So what's missing from our dream of living near water – and what's extra that might piss on our fireworks? Well, for a start living near water does mean it is damp. Now that's fine in the summer but come the winter it gets to be a real problem. How close to water you are will determine whether you run a serious risk of flooding. Some areas are particularly prone to flooding, and yet townies often view properties in summer and don't even check. One of our local villages has a banked up river, which floods every winter without fail, and alongside it there is an old terrace of cottages built *below* the level of the banks. The amazing thing is that people actually buy these houses, and then complain to the council when they flood.

A friend of mine had a country house once which had the river running through a culvert underneath it. Yes, it flooded every winter but there were flagstone floors and the water came in through the front door and out through the back door. Upstream they once had a yellow plastic duck race. They let hundreds of these ducks go, each with a number attached to its back. They promptly disappeared under the house and vanished. The organisers sent down a diver but he was unable to locate the missing ducks. Eventually after a week or two one bedraggled duck did reappear and someone was voted the winner. That winter, as the river levels rose, you could hear the ducks bobbling about in the brick culvert under the house when it was very quiet in the early hours of the morning. Quite eerie. Come the spring when the levels went down sufficiently they did all, one by one and very mildewy and decrepit, reappear but there was no one there to see their triumphant emergence into the sunlight once more.

On the Somerset Levels (and no doubt certain other places such as the Fens) the houses were designed to flood in winter. This went on as late as the mid 20th century, until the area was drained. As the weather turned in the autumn, all furniture and rugs were taken upstairs, where the family moved to for the duration. I once read an interview with a chap who had grown up like this. They used to moor their boat (their only transport) to the banisters, and fish for their supper from the landing. It wasn't hugely healthy, but they managed fine. Little surprise, then, that many houses on the Levels still flood every winter.

However, many houses which flood are impossible to sell. In areas where flooding is a worry, houses can sit on the market for years after flooding perhaps only once, many years ago. (Until a townie comes along, of course.)

Living near water often means you gain a lot of fair weather friends. They come down for the boating or the swimming or the beach parties when the sun is shining but you won't see 'em in the winter. (This, mind you, might be regarded as a bonus in some cases.)

We often make assumptions about what we are going to do to live out our dream without taking into consideration that everyone else might well be wanting to live out the same dream. I moved to Devon to be near water – the river Dart – and quite naturally bought a boat and expected to be able to rent a mooring locally. I was told I would have to wait for *dead-man's moorings*. Yes, you have to wait until someone literally dies for a mooring to become available. I bought a smaller boat which I tow to the water when I want to use it.

Oh, and another quick word about keeping boats. The amount of time you get to use them is much less than you would ever think and the amount of money you get to spend on them is much more than you'd ever think.

Whether you want to boat, fish, or sit by the river bank in the early evening, you won't be alone. Lots of wildlife also loves living in or near water – mosquitoes, midges, sea gulls (you have no idea how raucous and destructive they can be) to name but a few. The more boggy or wooded your stretch of river bank, the worse it will be for midges.

Perhaps you don't want rivers and lakes. Perhaps your dream is to live by the sea. Long walks on the cliffs, collecting driftwood along the tideline, skinny dipping at midnight. All of this is wonderful, but there are still downsides. If you live near the coast it can be pretty bleak in winter. The weather whips across, the rain drives at you and the view is grey. Beautiful and inspiring for a weekend maybe, but for months on end? You can't even get from the house to the car without getting soaked and frostbitten. Day after day after day. And the wild weather plays havoc with your garden. All that salt in the air means your choice of plants is severely limited. Fine if you're not a gardener, but depressing if you are.

But living near water is fun, beautiful, cathartic and ever changing. It is uplifting and relaxing, and there is *nothing* – absolutely nothing – half so much worth doing as simply messing about in boats. Whoops – a bit of personal bias creeping in there. OK, maybe for you fishing or sunning yourself on the beach are closer to your watery ambitions. But whatever your dreams of water, they can come true if you're wise to the drawbacks.

I know someone who reckons that the best way to live near water is to live on an estuary. This makes a lot of sense. You're protected from the harshest seaside weather, but you're bound to be close to the sea. The wildlife and the view is extremely varied and always present, and you can boat, fish or enjoy whatever riverside activities you please.

Pros

- If you enjoy fishing, boating, swimming in the sea, cliff walks or other water-related activities, they'll be right at hand if you live near water.

- The wildlife and the views are inspiring and relaxing to enjoy.

- You'll attract lots of visitors (if that's what you want).

Cons

- Flooding is a significant risk in many properties near water. And, to add insult to injury, insurance can be expensive or even non-existent in high flood risk areas.

- Even if it doesn't flood, it's generally damp. This may affect the house, or you may find damp weather affects your health.

- Boats are expensive, and if you don't have your own mooring you can't assume that there'll be one available nearby.

- If you fish, you may find that you get less time for it than you hoped. And you can't simply set up your rod and fish anywhere – you have to have a licence or a right to fish any particular stretch of water.

- Not all the wildlife is fun.

- Living by the sea can be terribly bleak and cold in the winter.

- Salty air by the coast makes gardening extremely challenging, and many of your favourite plants may simply refuse to grow.

- Living anywhere near water is always dangerous if you have small children, elderly folk or non swimmers. You cannot relax for a moment if the river runs through your property or the sea comes up to your front door.

- You have no control over what other people put in the sea or rivers. You can't assume any water will be safe or clean, and in some cases you can be quite sure it isn't. In some areas, Weill's disease is a significant risk.

Key Questions

- Do you want to own a stretch of water, or simply have it in your view? Or merely be in reach of it, such as a close drive to the sea?

- If you want to be by the coast, can you cope with the bleakness in winter? How long is winter in the part of the country you're looking in? Would you be better off a few miles inland?

- Is your dream property likely to flood? Badly? Will you be able to get affordable insurance?

- What are your water-related hobbies? Boating? Fishing? Check out how much these will cost, and whether you can easily get access, mooring rights, a fishing licence or whatever it is you need.

- How do you feel about mosquitoes? Most of us wouldn't cancel the dream of living near water just to avoid midges, but it might put you off buying somewhere right on the water's edge. Perhaps you'd be better off with a house a hundred feet up the hillside.

- Are you a keen gardener? Will you be able to grow the plants you want to near the sea, or in boggy ground?

- Is safety around water an issue in your household – are there children or non-swimmers? This may affect how close to water you choose to be.